THE FRIENDSHIP FORMULA

CAROLINE MILLINGTON is an award-winning journalist, author and media professional. She worked for national women's magazines for sixteen years before swapping print for digital. Caroline currently works at ITV.

This book belongs to...

Who is a fantastic friend because...

THE FRIENDSHIP FORMULA

Caroline Millington

HEAD
of ZEUS

An Anima Book

This is an Anima book, first published in the UK in 2019
by Head of Zeus Ltd

London Borough of Richmond Upon Thames	
RTTE	
90710 000 395 854	
Askews & Holts	
302.34 MIL	£10.00
	9781788545402

A catalogue record for this book is available from
the British Library.

ISBN (HB): 9781788545402
ISBN (E): 9781788545419

Printed and bound in Great Britain by
CPI Group (UK) Ltd, Croydon CR0 4YY

Head of Zeus Ltd
First Floor East
5–8 Hardwick Street
London EC1R 4RG

WWW.HEADOFZEUS.COM

In loving memory of Katie Haines

Contents

Contents

What is the Friendship Formula?

What makes a best friend? How do you cut out toxic people from your life? Who are the people you should surround yourself with to make you happy? Friendship feels like it should be easy, but the reality can be very different. If life was a pie chart, work and sleep would carve out big triangles, leaving you with a finite number of hours for family and friends – and deciding who you spend your precious free time with can sometimes feel more complicated than long division.

In my first book, *Kindfulness*, I wrote: 'Ultimately, we deserve to surround ourselves with cheerleaders, with people who support us, believe in us and are there in the good times and the bad. I think people fall into two categories: drains and radiators – they either suck us of energy and emotion or radiate warmth and love.' The Friendship Formula applies the concept of kindfulness* to friendship, in order to make sure you're getting the most out of all your relationships. It will help you to look at the drains and radiators in your life, and all the types of friendship in between. From who deserves to be in your close circle of friends to why friends are good for your health and how to cope with toxic fallouts.

As friends are the family we choose for ourselves, and female friendship feels more important than ever, the Friendship Formula celebrates the nurturing relationships we build together and helps us to cope when friendships break down.

---

* Kindfulness is blending mindfulness with being kind to yourself. Simply, remembering to treat yourself with kindness in all instances.

The basis of friendship – what we expect from friends and the way we deserve to be treated – is not bound by gender, sexuality, race or religion.

We'll be exploring the main aspects of friendship: the good, the bad and the ugly. The rise of the 'frenemy' and how to call them out on their behaviour; what to do if a friend 'ghosts' you; surviving friendship betrayal; and how falling in love and parenthood can impact on friendships. Can men and women ever just be good friends? Can you be friends with an ex? Is it ever a good idea to be friends with benefits? And the heart-breaking grief felt when a friend dies.

I hope the Friendship Formula will leave you wanting to tell your best friends how much you love and appreciate them, while accepting that some friendships naturally come to an end and the best thing to do is to let go and move on.

In *Kindfulness* I suggested you take a personal development review to look at all aspects of your life. You can use the Friendship Formula as an opportunity to do the same with your friendships. Just like Marie Kondo, the Japanese organizing consultant, has got us all going through our wardrobes, books and kitchen utensils (I mean, how many wooden spoons do we actually need?!), we should apply the same principles to our social circle.

Take ten minutes now to think about which friends bring you joy – the ones you want to spend more time with; who's lurking at the back of your closet, forgotten, and needs thanking for the lessons they've taught you before putting in your 'no longer bring me joy' pile?; and which mates need 'waking up'?

Hopefully, the Friendship Formula will help you look at the people around you, cherish the ones who bring you the most happiness, end those relationships which aren't good for you, motivate you to be open to meeting new people, and show you that spending time alone should be celebrated, not feared.

Ten Friendship Formula rules

1. Be the friend you wish to have.

2. Ditch toxic friends immediately and without hesitation.

3. Invest in the friendships that bring you the most joy and let others go with gratitude for the lessons they taught you.

4. Believe you deserve to be treated with respect and love by all your friends.

5. Recognize that falling in love and having children change friendships – but when you truly love a friend, you adapt and find the positives.

6. Accept that it's OK to let a friendship go, guilt-free, if it's run its course.

7. Love bomb your closest friends often and without reason.

8. Make the most of your work wives and husbands – they will make your work environment a happier place to be and can help develop your career.

9. Never hold onto a friendship out of a sense of duty.

10. Learn to enjoy your own company and find the positives in spending time alone.

'Women understand. We may share experiences, make jokes, paint pictures, and describe humiliations that mean nothing to men, but women understand. The odd thing about these deep and personal connections of women is that they often ignore barriers of age, economics, worldly experience, race, culture – all the barriers that, in male or mixed society, had seemed so difficult to cross.'

Gloria Steinem

Friendships: making you happy and healthy

I learnt what friendship is from my big sister, Leanne. The ultimate best friend, her honesty, kindness, loyalty and empathy know no bounds and have set a very high bar for any female friends in my life. From a young age, I expected people to make me feel the same way my sister did: safe, respected, cherished and entertained.

The next lesson I received in friendship was at school; when boys and girls could be friends but a game of kiss chase could confuse matters. My final childhood education on what I should expect from friendships came from books. Everything from *Winnie-the-Pooh* to *The Famous Five* gave me a clear idea of what friendship should be: adventures, moral support, fun and someone to lift you up when you're down.

I vividly remember Lucy Maud Montgomery's *Anne of Green Gables* novels and reading about Anne's best friend, Diana Barry, described as her 'bosom friend' and 'a kindred spirit'. It was the first time I had read something akin to sisterhood.

The Japanese have a term, *kenzoku*, which translated literally means 'family'. It suggests a bond between people who have a deep connection of friendship, who've made a similar commitment to each other and lived a shared history. Your closest friends, I learnt from a young age, should be the family you choose for yourself.

How do we find friends?

I wanted to find out how many people we meet in our lifetime and find out the number of potential friends we each have. Some say 10,000 while others estimate it could be up to 80,000 people!

Whatever the exact number, you're going to meet a lot more people that you *don't* end up being friends with than you *do*. So when it comes to making friends, here are my key ingredients...

History

There's a good reason why we stay in touch with people from school or university. You spend hours chatting about all the hilarious times you had together, reminiscing over the highs and lows, sharing memories and gossiping about where people are now. Beyond that, you might not have as much in common as you did when you swapped marbles and course notes. History can end up being the solid foundation of a good friendship.

Shared interests

If you're going to spend time with someone, it's clearly important that you like doing some of the same things – and a shared passion is always a good way to kick-start a friendship. Whether it's sport, films, politics, music or books, having a pastime you're both passionate about means you'll never run out of things to discuss.

Common values

I've met people who are 100 per cent my type on paper, but then they come out with a statement that stops me in my tracks. A homophobic aside, a sweeping generalization about the LGBTQ+ community, language I would never use to describe people of colour – and all respect goes out the window. Shared values and a moral code are the pillars of any friendship.

Equality

There has to be equality in a friendship – equal amounts of time sharing your good news and bad. Naturally, the need to be there for each other will ebb and flow, and life can throw a spanner (or a whole toolbox) in the works every now and again, but conversational hijackers must not be tolerated. If you only hear from someone when they need something, they are not a true friend.

A commitment to your happiness

Truth-tellers. 'Don't have a fringe cut, they just don't suit you.' 'He seems a great guy but since you've been with him you always talk about the issues you're having rather than the joy.' 'I love going out with you but you are a messy drunk at the end of the night and it spoils my fun.' The people who deliver opinions honestly but with kindness.

Being a good influence

They motivate you and bring out the best in you. Good friends challenge you to take risks and encourage you to fulfil your potential. They don't egg you on, don't mock you or belittle you in front of others. They are your best cheerleader.

Friendship is good for your health

We all know how important friendship can be – but it literally can be a lifesaver. In recent decades, there have been some groundbreaking studies into the importance of friendship and the impact it can have on our lives – and the dangers a lack of bonds and connections can have too.

In 2002, two women scientists at UCLA published a study on friendship among women, which claimed that stress can trigger a chemical reaction that causes women to make and maintain friendships with other women rather than triggering a fight-or-flight response. Previously, it was believed that men and women reacted to stress in the same way, but researchers believe that oxytocin is released as part of the stress response in women, which buffers the fight-or-flight response and, instead of preparing to fight or flee, encourages women to look after children and gather with other women instead. The action of 'tending or befriending' releases more oxytocin, which continues to calm the feelings of stress.

According to Drs Klein and Taylor, this calming response doesn't occur in men, because they produce high levels of testosterone under stress, which reduces the effect of oxytocin. So, when it comes to stress, 'Men walk, women talk.'

'There's no doubt that friends are helping us live longer,' Dr Klein has said. When women are

'I still have friends from primary school. And my two best girlfriends are from secondary school. I don't have to explain anything to them. I don't have to apologize for anything. They know. There's no judgement in any way.'

Emma Watson

feeling stressed they are more likely to turn to a female friend for comfort than walk away and say nothing. Sound familiar? I know in times of stress I'll put in an emergency call to a friend who'll soothe me with words of wisdom, offer gentle solutions or just listen as I offload.

In one 2017 study in America, researchers found that lonely people had a 50 per cent increased risk of early death, and in another study, those who had the most friends over a nine-year period cut their risk of death by more than 60 per cent.

According to a continuing study by Nurses' Health Study at Harvard Medical School that started in 1976, the more friends a woman had, the less likely they were to develop physical impairments as they aged. They were also more likely to be leading a joyful life. Research has shown that people with good friends often feel happier, less stressed and more like they belong than those without, and it's unsurprising to find experts saying that having a strong network of friends also increases self-confidence.

These researchers have also found that not having close friends or confidants is as detrimental to your health as smoking or carrying extra weight! Social ties reduce our risk of disease by lowering blood pressure, heart rate and cholesterol. People also take cues from their friends who exercise or eat well to lose weight and develop healthy habits, as claimed by a highly publicized 2007 study.

A study published in the *Australian and New Zealand Journal of Psychiatry* showed that increasing your level of social connection can protect your future mental health. We read so many articles about what we can do for our physical health, but an afternoon with our friends could be crucial to our mental health now and in the future.

A 2010 review of 148 studies found that people who felt less socially connected had more risk of early death than those who smoked, drank or were obese. Therapeutic programmes that focus on building social connectedness are effective in treating depression, anxiety and schizophrenia; and people who make new social group connections are less likely to develop depression.

The New Zealand Attitudes and Values Study (NZAVS) showed that, when a person's level of social connection goes down, they experience worse mental health a year later. However, there is some good news: the influence of social connectedness on mental health over time was about three times stronger than the other way around – the more social someone was, the more improved their mental health. All the more reason to spend time with the friends who make you happiest.

'My definition of a friend is
somebody who adores you even
though they know the things
you're most ashamed of.'

Jodie Foster

The Friendship Formula survey...

What traits do you look for in a friend?

'Kindness, honesty and fun.'

'Being reliable, understanding, clever, funny, enthusiastic and silly.'

'A good listener but doesn't judge. Someone who I can laugh with, but am not embarrassed to cry with.'

'No drama, fun, loyalty.'

'Trust, ability to listen, awareness of their own faults, sense of humour and no judgement.'

'Honesty, loyalty and acceptance.'

The Friendship Formula survey was conducted in 2019.

How to make friends

Stereotypes are lazy. When meeting someone new, it's too easy to stick labels all over them in some kind of Post-it-note-type frenzy. We can often be too quick to judge by appearance, accent or gender. We make assumptions about people based on the company they keep and where they work. Have a conversation and you might be surprised at how much you actually have in common. So when it comes to making new friends, keep an open mind and an open heart...

How to attract true friends

First rule: be the person you'd like to be friends with! You'll attract the people who share the traits you find the most appealing. Pursue your passions. Spend time doing what you like and you'll meet the right people for you along the way.

Making friends as an adult can be hard. When we're kids, it seems so easy. Our subconscious bias hasn't fully developed, and as long as the other kid is willing to share, we're friends – whether it's for two minutes in the park or for life. But finding new friends when you're older can be trickier.

A 2018 study from the University of Kansas revealed that time spent together is everything. Associate professor of communication studies, Jeffrey Hall, found that two people need to share fifty hours' worth of face time to turn from acquaintances to casual friends. After ninety hours spent together two people can become friends. They have to hit 200 hours together to qualify as close friends.

Spending 200 hours together doesn't actually mean you're guaranteed to become best friends.

'When you spend time joking around, having meaningful conversations, catching up with one another, all of these types of communication episodes contribute to speedier friendship development,' Dr Hall has said. 'You have to invest. It's clear that many adults don't feel they have a lot of time, but these relationships are not going to develop just by wanting them. You have to prioritize time with people.'

And hours spent working together doesn't count as much as quality time spent socializing. 'When people transition between stages, they'll double or triple the amount of time they spend with that other person in three weeks' time,' Dr Hall explained. 'We have to put that time in. You can't snap your fingers and make a friend. Maintaining close relationships is the most important work we do in our lives – most people on their deathbeds agree.'

As you get older, you'll probably find yourself with fewer close friends. A study in Finland in 2016 found that both men and women make more friends until the age of twenty-five. After that, the numbers begin to fall rapidly and continue to fall throughout the rest of our lives.

'We come from homes far from perfect,
so you end up almost parent and sibling
to your friends – your own chosen
family. There's nothing like a really loyal,
dependable, good friend. Nothing.'

Jennifer Aniston

The elusive 'F Factor'

We've established that spending time together creates close bonds and can turn an acquaintance into a close friend, but that's evidently not true of everyone we hang out with. Sometimes you click with someone, but often that spark is simply missing. What draws people together as friends – and keeps them close?

Proximity

According to those clever social psychologists, the proximity theory accounts for our tendency to form relationships with those who are close by – which makes total sense when you think how many hours you have to spend with someone before they become a friend. While you may be able to maintain a long-distance friendship, it's hard to form a bond with anyone you don't have regular face-to-face time with. The friends we make are often made at work (and transferred into after hours), on the same sports team, or with those who live close by. The proximity theory is also the reason you might meet someone who lives in another city or works for another company, who you know is a potential new best friend, but never quite get there.

Shared activities

You might not have as many extra-curricular activities in your diary once you've left school, but many close friendships are kick-started at some sort of club or group. Find a pastime you love and you'll meet like-minded people too: sports teams, book clubs, charity fundraising, a choir. You can't make new friends until you meet potential ones.

Common interests can be the most important ties that hold a friendship together because you commit to spend that time together. If either of you give up the activity, many see the friendship dwindle. While I met many of my closest friends through work, I also have a fabulous group of women in my life who I met through charity fundraising. Our friendship was a glorious surprise, as meeting new people wasn't the motivation to get involved. Now I can't imagine life without them. My advice: if you're looking to make new friends, start with volunteering for a local charity and you might just meet friends for life.

Go online

Forget dating apps for a minute, there are apps and websites where you can make friends too. Bumble BFF helps you meet like-minded people in your area. Peanut and Mush are both apps that connect mums. Meetup is also a great way to find people who share an interest in the same activity as you.

Life events

There are many events in life that either introduce you to new people or open up the possibilities of seeking out new friendships. Sometimes these are from a place of pain – a new job because you were made redundant, or the end of a relationship freeing up your evenings and weekends. Take the chance to turn something negative into a positive.

Starting a new job can be nerve-racking but it's also an opportunity to find new friends. Newly single? Throw yourself into doing all the things you never had time for – art classes, gin-tasting, stand-up comedy nights, evening classes – and you'll meet new people too. Happy occasions also give you a chance to broaden your social group – many of my mum friends have made brilliant mates at baby groups and at the school gates.

Thirteen Traits of Friendship

According to Professor Suzanne Degges-White, author of *Friends Forever: How Girls and Women Forge Lasting Relationships*, there are thirteen traits of friendship that fall into three categories: integrity, caring and congeniality.

Integrity is a core value cited as the bedrock of any relationship, and includes trustworthiness, honesty, dependability, loyalty and the ability to trust others. Basically, following your moral and ethical convictions to do the right thing. Meeting someone you believe has integrity makes you feel safe. Professor Degges-White also points out that caring – from empathy and listening to offering support and not being judgemental – is a key trait we look for in a friend. Finally, congeniality, which Professor Degges-White describes as self-confidence, humour and fun.

It seems three really is the magic number when

it comes to finding a friend. And there's no reason why you shouldn't have this list of traits in mind when 'auditioning' someone you've met as a potential friend. They might be fun and confident, but if they love to entertain a room and never stop to listen, are they going to offer you the friendship you deserve? Or they might have integrity but lack a sense of humour and just be too sensible for you.

Really, friendship is about two people each bringing half a jigsaw puzzle to the table and fitting their pieces together to make the perfect picture.

Auditions are open!

For me, finding people I have things in common with was easier when I was younger. You're on a similar path of discovery, finding out where you fit in the world. As we get older, we get stuck in our ways and seek like-minded people to complement us. I know these days I'm less likely to spend time with people I'm not emotionally invested in. I've definitely become more intolerant of people's nonsense and drama over the years, and have downsized my friendship group.

**Here are a few of my friendship rules –
feel free to add your own!**

**Never be embarrassed by your passions and
hobbies** – they will lead you to like-minded
people and potential new friends.

Put time and effort in. Keep in touch with regular texts and calls. Make your friends feel loved.
It takes seconds.

Ask yourself: who sees you when they have free
time and who frees up their time to see you?

Accept you're not a perfect friend. I know I've
disappointed people I love in the past and I'm
sure I've unintentionally hurt people's feelings
along the way. Be ready to say sorry to the
people you love.

Don't make false promises. If you bump into
someone you used to be close to, say how nice
it was to catch up but don't suggest meeting
up again out of politeness unless you mean it.

Accept that some people see you as an acquaintance when you'd like to be a friend. Unrequited friendship is painful but it's not you, it's them. Often it's simply a limitation of free time. And, ultimately, you only deserve people in your life who make you feel loved, secure and cherished.

'Friendship between women is different than friendship between men. We talk about different things. We delve deep. We go under, even if we haven't seen each other for years. There are hormones that are released from women to other women that are healthy and do away with the stress hormones... It's my women friends that keep starch in my spine and, without them, I don't know where I would be. We have to just hang together and help each other.'

Jane Fonda

The friendship circle

So, you've got your friends, gathered up over the years from a variety of places, but where do they all sit in your friendship circle? Your friendship circle can be impacted on by your lifestyle – a partner, children and other family members' needs can leave you with precious little time for friends. If you have a jug of time and people you care about holding out glasses waiting for you to fill them up, there's only so far your friendship supply is going to go. You choose wisely who to top up before refilling your jug and starting again the next day.

When I delved into the world of friends,

anthropologist Robin Dunbar from the University of Oxford seemed to be the most quoted expert on relationships, inclusive of friendships. In 1993, Professor Dunbar claimed that we can only maintain up to 150 significant relationships at the same time. He states these 150 people are the number of people you know and keep in contact with. It doesn't include people you've been friends with in the past but no longer have a social relationship with, or people you know but have no particular relationship with.

So, according to science, that's your limit: 150 people you may develop valued relationships with at any one time – but the depth of the friendship depends on which circle they are in. Many of them will be casual friends, the people you might invite to a big celebration like a wedding or milestone birthday. To be fair, you might even have more than 150 people in your life if you're particularly social!

The importance of the relationship increases as the number of people and size of circles decreases to the core people in your life, right at the centre. It's up to us who goes where. The outer circle is old school friends, people you once worked with, distant relations and friends of friends – people you'd want to get to speak to if you saw them. They might be on your Christmas card list but you don't confide in them or rely on them for your emotional well-being.

The next group of friends are the ones you're delighted to see at an event; you keep in touch at Christmas and maybe speak or get together a few times a year. There can be between thirty-five and fifty people in this circle. You see them as often as you can but you've no doubt uttered, 'We really must see each other more often' and then never do. You think of them as a good friend but they are yet to – and may never – become close.

According to Professor Dunbar, there are about fifteen people in the next circle – the friends you see once a month or so, known as the 'sympathy circle'. You're close friends, you can confide in them about most things, enjoy their company and can rely on them for support. You'd miss them if they weren't in your life and you make an effort to see them regularly.

Your smallest circle includes the friends you choose to see – or have some contact with – every week and are those you would turn to in a crisis. You invest more of your social time with these people than anyone else. These are your best friends and often include a family member or two, but there's a limit to how many close friends you can have in your inner clique at one time. According to one study, the average person manages just five close relationships at a time.

In 2007, Professor Dunbar and his colleagues analyzed phone records of 27,000 people in Europe and found that most people repeatedly interacted with the same four or five people in their phonebook. Professor Dunbar says these close relationships are limited in number because we are only able to fully invest and build connections with up to five people. If you're in a committed relationship, that person takes two places in your inner circle, leaving you with just the three close friends alongside your partner (more on this in Chapter 10!).

When it comes to the 150 people in your life, I believe it's pretty fluid. Different friendships fulfil different purposes and meet different needs. I know I have a handful of people I could turn to in a crisis but don't often speak to, let alone see every week! I also think I have a lot more than fifteen people in my 'sympathy' circle and fewer in my outer circle. You're either in or you're out!

According to Professor Dunbar, these numbers and proportions remain remarkably stable over time because membership moves between the circles. If a close friendship comes to a natural end or the person moves away, we'll simply slide a new person into the slot. Think of it like the Hunger Games for friendship!

Juggling friends

Some people actually wish they had fewer friends. The obligation to stay connected with people in our lives can be overwhelming. There can be a nagging guilt in not being a good enough friend and giving enough of your time or attention to everyone. But fear not.

A 2016 study found that only half of perceived friendships are actually mutual! I hate to be the one to break it to you, but many of the people you consider friends only think of you as an acquaintance, and there are probably many people you have happily popped into your outer circle of friends who think of you as one of their closest! That's right, up to half of our friendships are actually unreciprocated! So, as you move people between your circles, be prepared to be moved in and out of other people's. I think sometimes it happens due to circumstance, and can be subconscious or very much deliberate.

As you get older, your circles are likely to shrink. According to a study led by Cheryl L. Carmichael, we spend our twenties in 'identity exploration' mode. I'll put my hand up right now to spending my twenties dating unsuitable men, partying with some hardcore drinkers and trying to be friends with everyone I met along the way. My inner people-pleaser was more than happy to bend over backwards and make everyone else happy, while I seemed to forget to seek out what made me happiest. It's a decade spent trying to figure out who we are by socializing with lots of different people, exploring the different facets of yourself and seeing which feels the most like 'you'.

Once you're in your thirties, and perhaps forties, it seems we're settling into our true selves, and it's the quality of our socializing rather than the quantity that has a positive effect on our lives. If you follow the traditional life choices – marriage and children – this will naturally impact on how much time you have to spend with friends too.

Professor Carmichael has said: 'As individuals approach their thirties, social information-seeking motives wane. Identity exploration goals diminish with the transition into better-defined and more enduring social roles.' As we get older, our need to seek out new friends and experiences slows down. We know what we like and do more of the same rather than trying new things.

There are some big differences between my friendships in my twenties and thirties/forties…

- I've stopped being happy to crash on people's sofas and have started craving my own bed at the end of a night out.

- Nights out tend to end before midnight on a week night (most of the time!).

- Weekends away are spent with god-children as well as their parents – and

I'm just as happy staying in and catching up as I used to be going out.

- ◆ I spend less time with my 'party' friends and more time with people who like dinner with their alcohol.

- ◆ Brunch with the girls sometimes includes a baby or two in tow and we love it.

- ◆ Long-distance friendships are maintained by travel, social media, FaceTime and WhatsApp voice notes.

- ◆ I know when it's time to let a friendship go.

The circle of life

These are my kind of people. Genders are interchangeable, just see who fits into your circles...

The Twin

The person most like you – but that means they

may have your flaws too. You can clash but also be the closest. More like a sister, your bond is blood even though you're not related.

The SOS sister

Your 3 a.m. emergency contact. Your get-out-of-jail card. The one phone call you'd make when you're in trouble. Calm under pressure, cool in a crisis. You might not spend all your time together, but they've got your back.

The Prosecco and popcorn pal

It's not always deep and meaningful but they're your go-to person for fun nights out, healthy debate and the must-see movies. Reliable, trustworthy and always the first to book the latest event, we all need a go-to gig person in our lives.

The older and wiser woman

Need some sage advice, they're the one you turn to. Career, relationships, life choices – an older woman has been there, done that and bought the

T-shirt. She's also the one who checks in with you regularly just to see how you are.

The flighty friend

She floats in and out of your life, but that's just enough. You'd never give up your friendship even though you only catch up once in a blue moon.

The best bad influence

Has a heart of gold but always leads you astray. Whether it's one too many drinks, insisting you 'just put it on your credit card' or encouraging you to say yes to an unsuitable date, she's always up for some fun.

The school friend

You go waaaay back and they are the keeper of all your teenage secrets. You shared some of the big moments in life: first period, first snog, losing your virginity and learning how to mend a broken heart. There's a special soundtrack just for the two of you.

The adult friend

You met as grown-ups but bonded over being teenagers at heart. You cover every topic from Brexit to boys and bank balances (or lack of). You muddle your way through adulting together and are bonded for life.

The soul sister

Your everything. Your sister from another mister. She's your everything and life just wouldn't be the same without her.

The far-away friend

You met travelling or at work before one of you made the big move abroad, and now you're in different time zones with social media keeping you informed of each other's daily antics and the occasional FaceTime, making sure the bond stays intact. You invest enough to never give up on what you have, and on those rare occasions you do get to see each other in the flesh, it's like you've never been apart.

The hustler

Never stops; always trying new things. You admire their tenacity and fearlessness. In turn, they inspire you to take calculated risks, motivate you to have a 'can do' attitude and stop holding yourself back.

The cheerleader

The one you turn to when you need lifting up; when you just need chivvying along in life. They believe in you, your hopes and dreams, never question your ambition no matter how wild, and will do everything in their power to push you forward and fulfil your dreams.

The straight-talker

Everyone needs someone to tell it to them straight. But if you ask them if an outfit looks good, prepare yourself for an honest answer. They never make you feel bad on purpose but they always say it how it is.

Friendship later in life

According to new research, friends become increasingly important to health and happiness as people age. A 2017 study by William Chopik, assistant professor of psychology at Michigan State University, found that while both family and friend relationships were associated with better health and happiness, in older years the link only remained for people who reported strong friendships.

In a separate study of 7,500 older people in the US, he found that it wasn't just important to have friends – it was the quality of those friendships that was key. 'You have kept those people around because they have made you happy, or at least contributed to your well-being in some way,' he says. 'Across our lives, we let the more superficial friendships fade, and we're left with the really influential ones.'

So when you're looking to 'Marie Kondo' your friendship circles – looking at those who bring you joy and you want to keep, while thanking those who served a purpose and letting them go – know you are doing it to improve your quality of life, health and happiness!

Have a look in your phone and see – who are the five people you speak to and text the most? Do you consider them your closest friends?

If there's someone you love and notice you don't speak to as often, do you feel you should make more effort to keep in touch?

Write down the five people you're closest to. Now add the fifteen or so people you also consider close friends. Are there people on that list who you've drifted away from recently? Would you like to make more effort with them or consider if your relationship has maybe moved into an outer circle?

You might have a list of twenty people by now. Look at their names individually and consider the purpose of your friendship. Do they bring positivity to your life? Are they someone you trust? Or do you think you've been slack in your commitment to the friendship?

Now is the time to decide whether you want to re-commit to all these people. If you love them, take the opportunity to tell them! Send a text just to say you love spending time with them and value having them in your life. Or grab some cards and write a personal note – there's nothing like getting something in the post for no reason to make you feel loved.

Accept that some friendships may have shifted in the past year due to circumstances beyond your control. You don't have to have a big fall-out to fall apart. Trying to figure out when the right time to let go is? That's next...

'I'm so in love with her. She's proof that the love of your life does not have to be a man! That's the love of my life right there.'

Michelle Williams on Busy Philipps

The Friendship Formula survey...

What's the kindest thing a friend has ever done for you?

'Made me godmother to her boys!'

'Gathered me up after a massive breakup and moved me into their house for a bit.'

'Visited me daily when I was in intensive care.'

'Told me that my hairstyle (at the time) was so terrible that she was going to take me straight to a barber.'

'Let me live with her for free for six months.'

'Wrote a letter to tell me that they love being friends with me.'

'Attending my grandfather's funeral when she had never met him.'

'Put together a photo album of memories we shared over the years and wrote me the most beautifully wonderful letter.'

'Looked after me after the death of a boyfriend.'

'Lots of people want to ride with you on the limo, but what you want is someone who will ride the bus with you when the limo breaks down.'

Oprah Winfrey

What's a best friend?

'Best friends are people who help you.
They share and play with you. They help
you when you fall over. Best friends
should be kind. Yes, we fall out. We are
rude to each other sometimes. If we fall
out, we make up by saying, "I'm sorry".'
My niece Eliza, aged five

'A best friend should be someone who
understands you, gets your jokes and you
can have fun with. They would never spread
rumours about you and you should just be
able to be yourself around them. We just
hang out, make each other laugh and cheer
each other up when we're feeling sad. If we
fall out it's over some melodrama – we wait
for it to pass and then make up again.'
My goddaughter Jessica, aged fourteen

Best friends forever

When I was at junior school, I had a best friend called Zoe. When she left, she was replaced by Emily – we had sleepovers and went trick-or-treating together. Later, at my all-girls' senior school, I had a group of friends instead of one best friend, but I didn't really have a sense of belonging. There were girls I got on with really well, and I look back with fond memories of birthday sleepovers and lunchtime gossip, but the petty jealousies, fallouts and dramas were not for me. Making friends in my teenage years, I sometimes felt like Sandra Bullock in *Bird Box*: stumbling around with a blindfold on, desperate for human contact, not knowing who to trust and worried about getting hurt.

The first day of university was a turning point in friendships. After the initial introductions in halls we headed down to the first dinner. I remember the hall warden standing up declaring, 'Look around you now, because the person sat next to you will be your friend for life.' New housemate Ruth and I looked at each other with sheepish smiles, but that moment sealed the deal. She was my new best friend. And, while circumstance means we're not always at each other's side, we're best friends for life.

As I've said, my sister Leanne has set a high bar when it comes to friendship. She's my ultimate ride or die. So my closest friends – men and women – are all epic people who hold a special place in my heart.

With my BFF Ruth, we don't see each other as much as we'd like due to distance and family – her brilliant husband and two boys – but we continue to invest in our friendship. We've been through a lot together: breakups, bereavements, marriage, children, career issues, health scares and more. Our friendship is totally different to how it

'The friends with whom I sat on graduation day have been my friends for life. They are my children's godparents, the people to whom I've been able to turn in times of trouble, friends who have been kind enough not to sue me when I've used their names for Death Eaters. At our graduation we were bound by enormous affection, by our shared experience of a time that could never come again, and, of course, by the knowledge that we held certain photographic evidence that would be exceptionally valuable if any of us ran for prime minister.'

J. K. Rowling

was in our university years because our lives have taken different paths, but we share more than just history.

I think friendship is a bit like taking part in *Strictly Come Dancing*: you need clear communication, patience, endurance, trust, kindness and compromise. You take it in turns to lead – when one can't see the direction you're going in, the other guides the way. Sometimes you break apart for a solo moment, but you always come back together and you always forgive each other for the occasional misstep and mistake.

While the best friendships are equal, the reality is they're not 50/50 all the time. Sometimes you rely on the person more, or they lean on you, but, ultimately, it's a partnership. In fact, your best friend could end up being the love of your life. Over half of Brits aged 25–44 are now single and, according to the Marriage Foundation, half of millennials in the UK will never get married. Best friends have never had such an important role in our lives.

New research conducted by the personalized gifting website The Book of Everyone asked 1,027 women aged sixteen and over about their closest female friendships and found that on average a UK woman has six significant female friendships throughout her life and that women spend 67 per cent more time improving their romantic relationships compared to their friendships – and 30 per cent of women are more likely to cancel plans with their best friend than with their boyfriend or girlfriend. Ouch! This research also found that the average female friendship span for women in the UK is sixteen years – six years longer than the average romantic relationship.

Despite what we've seen about the growing importance of female friendship, it seems some women haven't got the memo yet.

The recipe for friendship

The following are my must-haves for close friendships:

Kindness

The number one attribute we all look for in a

friend. A friendship will not prosper and grow without simple acts of kindness.

Honesty

You should be able to tell your best friend anything and expect an honest answer, delivered with kindness. If their idea of honesty is too brutal, you can ask them for a more tactful view!

Give and take

In an ideal world, the effort put in by both friends should be 50/50, but we don't live in an ideal world. Sometimes it will be up to you to make more effort and invest time in your friendship. The ebb and flow of a friendship is natural, but always keep an eye out in case you get stuck in giving 80 per cent for too long. If you begin to feel taken for granted, it's up to you to communicate your needs.

Communication

From keeping in touch and making each other

feel wanted to resolving any conflict, sorting out your differences and learning to talk about your needs. Lack of communication – and a hesitation to express disappointment or hurt – seems to be one of the main reasons friendships fall apart. Better to talk things through with kindness at the heart of the matter than let things fester and see a friendship turn sour, leaving both parties confused and frustrated at where it all went wrong.

'I don't know what I would have done so many times in my life if I hadn't had my girlfriends. They have literally gotten me up out of bed, taken my clothes off, put me in the shower, dressed me, said, "Hey, you can do this," put my high heels on and pushed me out the door!'

Reese Witherspoon

Shared humour

This is the basis of so many close friendships – the same outlook on life, finding the same things funny, but never making the other person the butt of a joke.

Dependability

You can rely on each other and trust their word. You know they won't let you down at the last minute without a valid reason or explanation.

Independence

Your lives complement each other, running in parallel, but you're not co-dependent. It's important to develop your own self-worth and not purely validate yourself through friendship.

The recipe for a perfect friendship doesn't actually exist – it's unique to you! Your needs and priorities are different to mine and everyone else's, and over time our friendship needs may change too.

Male bonding

Forget sports chat over a pint, close heterosexual male friendships go way beyond superficial conversation and bravado. There was a time when men were expected to be the strong, silent types, back-slapping their affections and competing for jobs and women.

I believe men, in this century, enjoy authentic and deep friendships with their guy friends, and there's never been a more important time for this. According to researchers from the University of Winchester, young men get more emotional satisfaction out of close heterosexual friendships than romantic relationships with women. Participants in the 2017 study said they felt less judged by their bromances than by their girlfriends, and that it was easier for them to overcome conflicts and express their emotions to a close guy friend than to a love interest.

Adam White, a researcher at the University of Winchester and lecturer in sport and physical education at the University of Bedfordshire, said: 'This is potentially a really significant shift in young men's behaviour, recognizing they now may be able to talk, share and support each other with a whole host of physical and mental health vulnerabilities. Unfortunately, while positive for men, this may disadvantage girlfriends and traditional relationships, which are seen as having more pressures and regulation. These men told us how they would often prioritize their bromantic relations over their romances. So, if guys can now get all of the benefits from their bromances, it reduces male to female relations to sex.'

Professor Eric Anderson, a professor of sport, masculinities and sexualities at the University of Winchester, added: 'The rise of the bromance is directly related to the diminishment of homophobia. It signals that young, straight men no longer desire to be trapped by older, conservative notions of masculinity.'

It appears that friendships for both men and women are evolving and becoming more important than ever.

'He's a great actor, a great man and I'm glad to call him my friend.'

Tom Hiddleston on Benedict Cumberbatch

'You can tell we really like each other. We really are friends, and we're giving each other crap like we've known each other all our lives. I just think the world of that dude.'

Blake Shelton on Adam Levine

'Other women who are killing it should motivate you, thrill you, challenge you and inspire you rather than threaten you and make you feel like you're immediately being compared to them.'

Taylor Swift

Work friends and foes

F riends at work are like a good bra: they perk you up, make you look good and always support you!

You can spend over forty hours a week in the company of people you wouldn't actually choose to. According to LinkedIn's Relationships@Work study in 2014, 46 per cent of professionals world-wide believe that work friends are important to their overall happiness. In my experience, having friends at work can be a game changer. Jobs I've had working alongside great friends have been a joy while being in an office without close mates has left me feeling isolated and unsupported. But beware the millennial mate looking to further their career. When asked whether they would sacrifice a work friendship for a promotion, 68 per cent of millennials said they would. Savage!

However, there appears to be a huge difference in attitudes towards friends at work across the generations. When it comes to baby boomers (aged 55–65), 45 per cent of professionals said that such friendships had no effect on workplace performance. It seems older people see the workplace as functional and don't look for emotional bonds with co-workers. However, this generation shows more loyalty to friends, with 62 per cent of boomers saying they would never even consider sacrificing a friendship for a promotion. In another survey of 4,000 employees and 100 employers by Total Jobs, it was revealed that just 17 per cent of us have a best friend at work. I think this is such a shame as becoming close to a work colleague can be beneficial on so many levels.

Having a close friend at work can save your sanity and career, although in my experience, when a friendship in the office turns sour, it can do the exact opposite. The workplace can be a stressful environment at the best of times, so finding 'your people' in the office can feel like winning the lottery – but work-centred friendship comes with a whole host of complications too.

I've been lucky enough to pick up some of the very best people throughout my career and carry the friendship out the door along with my P45. But for every person I've grown close to at work and developed a personal friendship that goes beyond the canteen, there are many that I haven't.

Becoming friends with someone at work can give you a false sense of kinship. The bond is built purely on what you have in common in the workplace and doesn't go beyond the confines of the office. Finding someone who really gets you can make or break a job.

Like having your own emotional support peacock, a best friend at work helps you deal with stress. It can be difficult managing emotions and often our job is the one place that triggers the most emotional reactions. In the past, I've struggled with anxiety in the workplace and it was the support of a close friend who got me through. They knew the people I was dealing with, the management and structure. There was no second-guessing behaviour or assuming I was being over-sensitive. They could be there for me because they saw it first-hand.

> **What you get from good work friends:**
>
> * Lunch companion.
> * Shoulder to cry on.
> * Telling you when your eye make-up has smudged or you have something in your teeth before a big meeting.
> * Someone to take your side when your boss is being an idiot.
> * Cries when you tell them you want to leave your job but encourages you to do it anyway because they want the best for you.
> * A tea and coffee buddy.
> * Emergency tampon supplies.

More than just (work) friends

According to LinkedIn's 2014 Relationships@ Work study, office-based friendships are changing: 67 per cent of millennials are likely to share personal details including salary, relationships and family issues with co-workers, compared to only about one third of baby boomers.

Building personal relationships at work can help us feel connected, making us more motivated and productive – but how do you move a work friend into 'real life', from professional to personal?

Make sure you're on the same page and try not to take offence if they'd rather keep your friendship to office hours only. A friend of mine was shocked when someone she worked with suggested they spend the day together at the weekend. They got on, but as far as my friend was concerned, it was a work-based bond. Remember, just because you get on well with someone, doesn't automatically make them a friend. It took me a long time to get my head around that and realize that, sometimes, you have to accept your place in the friendship circle the other person puts you in!

If you find you have a million things in common beyond your boss, suggest an outing that's related to your shared interests – a film, sports event or gig. You'll know after spending time together outside work if you're meant to be more than just office buddies. Pick your work friends wisely: you don't want someone who will repeat a confidence so you become office gossip.

The 'work wife'/'work husband'

Many people refer to their closest friends in the office as their 'work wife' or 'work husband'. I've had a few 'work brothers' too.

Take Nick for example. The first time I met Nick, it didn't go well. He loves to regale people with the fact that I was mean to him the first day we worked together. I made a sarcastic comment that went down like a cup of sick – and I've been trying to make up for it ever since! There's nearly a decade age gap but it makes no difference – he's my little brother from another mother, my favourite person to fly with and one of my most trusted friends. Because he forgave the terrible start to our friendship (I'm sorry, Nick!), we bonded over our love of strong tea, Pink and travel.

I found a 'work wife', Jessica, in another office. We bonded over our love of Taylor Swift and nineties movies, and our friendship has flourished through a number of job changes (mine) and a wedding and a baby (hers), because there is so much more to us than the environment we worked in.

I've worked with hundreds, if not thousands of people. I didn't like everyone I shared office space with and I'm sure there were plenty of people who didn't think I was their cup of tea either. And that's fine. When your work relationship ends, a true friendship should continue out in the real world. It's no longer fuelled by office gossip, unrealistic deadlines and comparing hangovers after too much Prosecco at the Christmas party. It's about making the effort to meet up and invest time in each other's lives.

Beware the false work friend

At one point in my career it was a daily ritual to hit the pub afterwards. We'd head to the nearest overpriced bar or pub and dissect the day, moaning about management and bitching about things going wrong. It turned out to be the worst practice. Instead of leaving office issues where they belonged, the group thrashed them out for hours. There was no time to decompress. Those precious hours that should be for relaxing and thinking about anything but work were saturated with office drama – and what can happen in these situations is an implosion. Bitching. Infighting. People taking sides. Friends refusing to take sides. Never mind the celebrity dramas we were writing about, the office turned into a daily soap opera.

Be mindful of the time you spend with people from work and the conversations that take place. Any issues that arise after one too many drinks can spill back into the work environment and make for awkward meetings. You don't need to share your personal life with everyone at work so set clear boundaries, even in social situations.

Know who you can trust, and don't get drawn into any conversation you're not comfortable with. The last thing you need is someone repeating a private pub conversation in the workplace and it having a negative impact on your career.

Work friendship rules:

* Remember your friendship will last longer than the job you are in.

* Treat each other with respect.

* Don't take office politics out of the building, enjoy the time you spend together outside of work and don't discuss anything to do with your job.

* Set boundaries on how you treat each other in the workplace – over-familiarity between friends can lead other people to thinking they can speak to you and treat you in the same way. I had a 'no swearing until after 6 p.m.' rule which helped!

* If someone asks lots of questions but doesn't give away much about themselves, be wary.

* Enjoy your friendship but be mindful of excluding others. You don't want to be thought of as cliquey.

The Friendship Formula survey...

How has a 'work wife' or 'work husband' supported you?

'I was feeling very lonely after my son was born, as a single mum of two children. My 'work husband' took me out to the cinema, called over with junk food and movies. It later bloomed into a romance and we now have a child, and he's about to become a real husband!'

'I had a tough time last year, I was going through a lot of shit. She always sent me little messages, and even sent me your first book, *Kindfulness*, as a surprise in the post once!'

'When I had a disagreement with my boss over my contract, she was there to make light of it and help me feel less anxious.'

'I think you should embrace every friendship that you come across, especially at work. We spend so much time there, we need to have those friendships to keep us human.'

'I've sat next to the same person at work for the last ten years, so she's definitely my 'work wife'. We chat all day and I tell her things that I wouldn't tell some of my closest friends. We have similar personalities and have got each other through incredibly tough times at work and in our personal lives. We've worked together for a long time and I know her probably as well as I know my best friends outside work.'

'I do believe that female friends can be worse to each other than male friends, simply because, for whatever reason, women have a stronger emotional language. We're encouraged more to use that... We talk about what we're feeling about deep things. Maybe they're not even particularly deep, in the grand scheme of things, but they're things that matter to us. So, when you give someone that power, you're showing them where your buttons are. If you pick wrong, and someone turns around and short-circuits those buttons, I think it hurts more.'

Anne Hathaway

Letting go of a friend

It's over. Sometimes it fizzles out or disappears so slowly you barely notice; at other times there could be a major drama that sees a shock end. There's no way we can carry every friend we ever make through our lives with us. Remember that magic number, 150? As new people come into our lives, something – or someone – has got to give. We make way for new friends, the ones who really do bring us joy, by letting go of others.

It can be both liberating and unsettling as your friendship circle shifts. Adulting often feels like a never-ending quest to please others, but there is one person who you should be putting before anyone else: yourself. It can be painful to see friendships sacrificed, bonds broken, feelings discarded, but along the way you'll make new friends and invest in people you have more in common with.

Why do friendships change – and how do we let go of good people, guilt-free?

Breaking up is hard to do

Often friendships fade away because of a lack of balance. We all know that the best kind of friends reciprocate the time, energy and dedication we put in. When it feels off-kilter, it can really challenge your commitment.

As our lives take different paths – careers, relationships, travel, children – friendships come under pressure, and it takes effort on both sides to continue. While we once had everything in common, changing lifestyles can dramatically impact on people's availability and means to do things together.

Even if you continue to spend time together, one or both of you may grow frustrated at the quality of the experience. You can both end up feeling taken for granted. There have been times when I've felt like I'm going through the motions in a friendship rather than relishing it, which leaves me feeling confused and questioning my worth. Long-term friendships may grow in parallel, closer, or apart. The things that drew us together in the first place may no longer exist. That magic connection dissolves over time. Unlike marriage, we never exchange vows with our best friends. It's an unspoken promise to be in each other's lives – and we're not obligated to friends the same way we are to our partners or even family members.

Friends are elastic and friends won't hold you back from falling in love, pursuing your career or travelling abroad. Best friends support each other in their life choices, even when it means you won't see as much of them anymore. Because best of friends – the ones whose hearts are truly connected – never lose their bond.

Friendships ebb and fade with frequency. A 2009 study by sociologist Gerald Mollenhorst found in a seven-year period most people had replaced half of their friends, with only 30 per cent of close friends remaining so. Sometimes, however, friends drift apart, consciously or not.

Distance

Physical and emotional. You can have a BFF at work one minute but, when one of you leaves, you realize the friendship never actually went much deeper than office talk. Yes, you talked about your personal life and problems over lunch, but when it came to getting a date in the diary one night after work, neither of you got round to it.

Other mates might move to another town – or even country – and while you stay in touch on social media, visiting them is just not a priority and the friendship slowly fizzles down to Christmas cards. They've naturally moved from your inner circle to the outer one. Neither of you are hurt by this, it just seems like a natural progression.

Friendships sometimes slip away from us so unexpectedly and quietly we don't even notice, and then when we do, it feels like too much time has passed to reach back and grasp them by the hand. We're all guilty of maintaining a friendship for history's sake. You're not emotionally invested in them but can't bring yourself to cause a fuss and cut ties, especially if they are part of a bigger friendship group.

Money matters

When it comes to friends, financial imbalance can play a part in a relationship shift. Money – or lack of it – can cause a huge issue in friendships.

One UK survey found that half of 'low earners' have cancelled plans with friends because they worried it would end up being too expensive, and 39 per cent of 'high earners' have deliberately stopped spending time with people because of financial incompatibility. In fact, the same survey found that half of the 'high earners' look for friends who earn a similar amount of money to them, while lower earners revealed that money had more impact on friendships than geographical distance, difference in politics or having children. So, the payday problem can be a serious one.

In the UK, revealing what you earn is still fairly taboo. According to the survey, it's even more taboo for women: 80 per cent say they've avoided discussing their salary with family and friends, while 32 per cent feel uncomfortable talking about it altogether. I don't know what my friends earn, but I was shocked by the results of the survey and the impact your salary can have on mates.

Money does impact on friendships to some degree, and when planning time together it can play a huge factor – but, for me, friendship is worth more than any amount in the bank. We've all had that one friend who found themselves earning more than others and moved into a different network of friends who can afford to splash their cash. Ultimately, though, it's all about compromise and communication. If money is tight, tell your friends you haven't got much spare cash and suggest a free-ish fun challenge – each take it in turns to organize a get-together for under a set amount of money each. Or let friends know you're short on cash before you book a dinner – take control and decide on a cheap and cheerful venue. Better still, if you're able to play hostess, cook a budget dish and ask everyone to bring a bottle.

When it comes to birthdays, true friends would rather spend time with you than have expensive gifts. A small, meaningful gift is better than money splashed on something fancy with no thought behind it. Get creative. Some of my favourite presents have been paintings, a book with a heartfelt message written inside or a home-made cake. Love doesn't cost a thing.

When the pay gap becomes glaringly obvious in a friendship, acknowledge it but don't make it a big deal. Either of you can feel awkward if it keeps rearing up as an issue, but investing in your friendship is more important than the amount of money you spend when you're together. We all go through periods when we have more or less cash to play with, so treat your friends when you can.

Friendship fallouts

In 2017, a study of 2,000 UK adults found that the average person has sixteen friends and acquaintances – but they don't actually like three of them! Which explains why they're let go from the friendship circle.

The survey found these were the top fifteen reasons we don't like our own friends:

1. Having nothing in common.

2. Being too bossy or controlling.

3. A difference of opinions.

4. How they behave when they've been drinking.

5. Being too high-maintenance.

6. Leading different lifestyles.

7. Use of language.

8. They've let you down.

9. Sense of humour.

10. How they treat their partner.

11. They've changed.

12. Political affiliations.

13. How they treat their children.

14. Not liking the people they hang out with.

15. Being blanked by them.

When I look at this list, I see some issues that can be talked through and resolved and others that are too toxic to have in your life. So, what to do when you find yourself in this predicament?

Deciding to let go!

Ask yourself the following questions when considering letting a friendship go:

- What is the purpose of this friendship?

- Are they a good friend to you?

- What has changed?

- Are you both responsible for the change?

- Do you want to put more effort in or can't be bothered?

- Can the friendship grow?

- Do you miss them if you don't see or hear from them for a long time?

- How do you feel at the thought of only keeping in touch casually – upset, relieved, guilty?

- Are you ready to let the friendship go?

You might find that there's a lack of time but you don't want to give up on the friendship. Speak to your friend and say something like, 'We don't have enough free time to see each other as much as I'd like, but let's try to get something in the diary and make sure we catch up as regularly as we can.' You're committing to the friendship even if it's only once or twice a year. That might be enough for you both. Or you might realize you don't even want to broach the subject, and while you wish them well, you don't miss having them in your life. Give yourself permission to let them go, guilt-free!

The *Kindfulness* guide to friendship

Allow yourself to phase out a friendship if you no longer think you have anything in common. Do you feel you should maintain a friendship but not sure how? Suggest things you like to do – trip to the cinema, day out at a theme park, spa day, shopping – and if they're not interested, take it as an opportunity to mention that you don't seem to have much in common any more.

If a friend always feels the need to control your time together – picking the activity or venue, times and who can or can't join you – it can really take its toll. If you want to salvage the friendship, organize some time together without their input; if they object or try to take control, take the opportunity to explain that you BOTH need to decide on plans. In my experience, friends who need to control the time you spend together suffer from anxiety or lack of self-confidence, so it's always worth broaching their mental health too.

Suggest group activities with other mutual friends and stop seeing them one-on-one. This might be enough for you. Take a moment to notice your friendships and if you've been shifted from one circle to another without realizing. Don't take this personally – especially if it hadn't occurred to you until now! – but respect the person's boundaries and enjoy any time you do spend with them.

I've seen friendships ebb and flow. I've lost friends because of silly mistakes and a lack of communication. I've watched as friends edge out of the room slowly, backing away from the bond we once had. At other times, I've been so caught up in my own life I've turned around and realized a friend is no longer there. They got up and left, and I didn't notice.

How to deal with losing a friendship

It's only natural to feel sad or upset, but accept that people come into our lives for a reason – sometimes to teach us something or introduce us to a new way of looking at life. The friendship may be over, but carry with you any life lessons you've picked up along the way.

Accept that the friendship is over but allow yourself to look back at the good times and feel happy.

Look at the friendships you do have and what you love about them. Surround yourself with positive people who you enjoy spending time with.

If you're still friends with them on social media, allow yourself to unfollow them or – if you're worried about blocking them – simply mute their account so it doesn't show up in your feed.

You can still want the best for someone even if you don't want them to play a big part in your life any more. Don't beat yourself up about it. If you miss them but you simply drifted apart rather than had an epic fallout, feel free to send a Christmas card and update them with your news from the year, tell them you think of them and wish them well.

It's important to remember, you might grow apart from a friend for a while, but sometimes life draws you back together again. If there's been no toxic breakup, I think it's a good idea to keep the door to friends open and let each other come and go as much as you both want.

If you feel like you've neglected a friendship and it fizzled out because you didn't put enough effort in, don't be too embarrassed to get in touch. Send a card in the post saying, 'Saw this and thought of you' or a text. If you don't hear back, they've clearly moved on with their life, but you have nothing to lose.

'Learning the difference between lifelong friendships and situationships: Something about "we're in our young twenties!" hurls people together into groups that can feel like your chosen family. And maybe they will be for the rest of your life. Or maybe they'll just be your comrades for an important phase, but not forever. It's sad but sometimes when you grow, you outgrow relationships. You may leave behind friendships along the way, but you'll always keep the memories.'

Taylor Swift

The Friendship Formula survey...

Have you ever let a friendship fade out?

'Plenty of times! I'm a real believer that you have friends for reasons, seasons and forever. Most of the time I let it go. People will come back into your life if they're meant to.'

'Distance has made friendships fade. I feel I am still holding on to my best friend from secondary school but do wonder if we'd be friends if we met today.'

'Yes, a very good friendship lasting five years simply faded out when I found a new career and she found a new friendship group who prefer to party.'

'More so as I've got older – I think I'm more accepting of it now. Just because you lose touch, doesn't mean it wasn't a successful or worthwhile friendship.'

'In the past I tried to force it to continue, now I just let it fade out. You can only have so many meaningful friendships.'

'If friends disappoint you over and over, that's in large part your own fault. Once someone has shown a tendency to be self-centred, you need to recognize that and take care of yourself; people aren't going to change simply because you want them to.'

Oprah Winfrey

Toxic fallouts

We've looked at friendship circles and letting friendships go when they naturally fizzle out – but have you noticed any red flags? The toxic.

It's time to take an inventory of your own friendships. Negativity in friendships is unhealthy, and it's important to recognize the signs so you can either make changes or end the friendship for good. Yes, there are ups and downs and even disagreements and fallouts, but conflict shouldn't be central to any relationship. If there are people in your life who regularly upset you, make you question your self-worth, put you down or try to control you, it's time to step away.

Brexit. Boyfriends. Booze. Bullying. There are many catalysts that can cause the toxic end of a friendship. You may have once enjoyed a balanced and healthy friendship, but sometimes people change and if you're no longer enjoying a fulfilling and happy relationship you have to give yourself permission to put your own needs first and walk away.

If you're thinking about some particular friends in your life, here are a few things to consider:

You do NOT have to agree with your friend on everything

Many of my friends have different views to me on politics and religion – two topics that are notoriously controversial – but we can still enjoy discussing them because we respect each other. Debating and discussing contentious issues can help you see another point of view, expand your knowledge and reinforce your viewpoint. Be willing to listen. Talk about it reasonably and feel free to agree or disagree. Remember, surrounding yourself only with people who agree with all your opinions can create an echo chamber – and is quite frankly boring! But don't allow someone to belittle your beliefs.

What are your friendship deal-breakers?

While you might be able to remain close with a friend who votes differently to you, what are your deal-breakers? You might be mates for years, when a news story throws up a controversial subject you don't agree on. You can quickly agree to disagree and move on, but know where your boundaries are. For me personally, I've called friends out on racism and homophobia – and, yes, it changed my opinion of them and I distanced myself from them too.

Moral dilemmas

Some of the most important friendships in my life have ended not because of distance or lack of time but a dynamic shift in the other person's life. There was a friend who distanced herself from me, leaving me hurt and bewildered. It turned out she'd had stuff going on in her personal life she thought I'd judge her on. She was wrong and had cut me off for no reason. Another friendship came crashing down because she had left her partner for someone else but continued to lie to her ex about the new relationship for months. The situation made me into a liar and I lost all respect for the way she was treating her ex. Know your boundaries. It's not about judging other people, but if friends act in a way that makes you uncomfortable you are entitled to a) call them out on it and b) walk away from the friendship guilt-free.

Frenemies and signs of a toxic friendship

It can start small. A little retort that throws you but is followed up with a smile, leaving you confused. Did your friend just diss you or are you being 'oversensitive'? As someone who has been described as 'too sensitive' by people in the past (and it wasn't meant as a compliment), I believe that it's a lazy, rude and demeaning way to dismiss a friend's feelings.

I've learnt that I might be sensitive, but if friends feel the need to point this out, they also need to take a long, hard look at their behavior which is provoking my sensitive and emotional response. In my experience, friends have been very happy to enjoy the benefits of my sensitivity – the ability to feel a shift in their mood, an empathetic ear when they want to offload, a soothing counselling session when times are tough – but on a couple of occasions my feelings have been all too easily dismissed.

If friends are happy to enjoy the best side of your sensitivity, they should also respect the emotional side that comes with it. People misspeak and often it's without malice, but if you notice a pattern of behaviour from a friend in which you feel like they are putting you down, dismissing your opinions or ideas, quashing good news with their own, or clearly questioning life decisions you have full confidence in, it's time to take a good look at that person and decide if having them in your life brings you happiness.

If anyone makes you feel diminished, belittled, used or humiliated, you need a serious conversation with them about their behaviour and how it makes you feel, or you need to walk away. Often this kind of toxic behaviour is fuelled by jealously and resentment – classic frenemy traits.

The Urban Dictionary defines a frenemy as: 'A person in your life (usually friend of friend or co-worker) who you get along with and whose overall company you enjoy but who will cut you down at virtually any opportunity with mostly backhanded compliments or jabs. Always roots for you to do good but just not better than them. Normally stems from some jealousy to any or all aspects of your life.' Sound familiar? Yep, me too.

My rule is to give them one chance. Have a conversation about how one example of their behaviour made you feel and explore it with them. If that behaviour doesn't change, make a conscious decision not to spend time with them. People often aren't aware of how hurtful their actions and words can be when they are so caught up in their own pain, and sometimes pointing out that what they said was hurtful and rude can be enough of a wake-up call to stop the behaviour and get your friendship back on track.

Signs of a toxic friend

Confused about whether a friend's behaviour is toxic or just a bit off? Consider the following...

They ask to catch up but spend the whole time talking about themselves and showing no interest in you. Their personal psychodrama is intense and you keep being pulled into it, leaving you drained and frustrated.

Shows little sympathy for your problems and is likely to hijack an issue as their own, explaining they're going through the same thing only a million times worse.

Only sees you on their terms – as and when it suits them with little regard for you, making you feel like you revolve around them.

There's an ongoing joke and you're the punch-line. Even when you don't laugh or explain that you don't find it funny, they keep the joke going at your expense in front of others.

They put you down: your choice in partners, TV shows, hobbies or clothes. Sometimes it can be really subtle: 'You like that? Really? OK...', leaving you wondering if you're over-analyzing what that meant. If this is a constant in your friendship, they are undermining your decision-making and wearing down your self-confidence.

They put down other friends of yours, making it difficult for you to socialize together as a group and leaving you feeling very awkward.

They sabotage your happiness by making you doubt yourself. Rather than supporting a new health kick, career change or relationship, they encourage you to rebel, cheat, take a day off, not tie yourself down, just be happy with what you've got. 'You used to be so much fun/don't be boring,' etc.

Co-dependent friendships that turn toxic

Many of the friendships I've experienced or witnessed that turned sour have been co-dependent. By that I mean, one party is the 'taker' – often bouncing from one life crisis to another, something of a drama queen/king, and demanding attention – while the other person is a 'giver', who takes on the role of a rescuer to the extreme of becoming a martyr and thriving off being needed.

While this kind of friendship can happily last for years with both people satisfied and fulfilled by their roles, it can also come to a head. The 'taker' may experience some personal growth that leads to a less dramatic lifestyle, leaving the 'giver' feeling unwanted and no longer needed. Or the 'giver' could begin to feel that the support only goes one way and starts setting boundaries that the 'taker' doesn't like.

Givers can begin to suffer from 'compassion fatigue' where they feel put-upon and exhausted by supporting others; they may realize they need help to be more assertive in friendships, validating themselves rather than relying on being needed by others to make them feel good about themselves.

Sometimes there can be a fallout between the friends when they don't feel their needs are being met – I've witnessed a 'taker' move on and find another 'giver' friend, while the 'giver' finds a new 'taker' friend in crisis to support. Sadly, it's a cycle of behaviour not often recognized by those personally involved until one of them may decide to enter counselling or therapy and recognizes repetitive behavioural patterns they can change.

Either way, it's not the healthiest of relationships and both people should recognize that and move it onto a more equal footing, being there for each other in times of need.

Having a difficult conversation

You've got something you need to get off your chest but you don't know how to say it. Broach a difficult conversation with kindness at the heart of it and a clear intention to set a boundary. Try: 'You know the other day when you said/did xxx? I actually found it hurtful. I wanted to find out what motivated you to say/do it, so we should talk it over and clear the air.'

By starting the conversation like this, you're calling them out on their behaviour but clearly stating you want to discuss it and still be friends.

No doubt they might be defensive, but a real friend will hear you say you're hurt, and apologize. You can call attention to their behaviour without punishing them and open up a dialogue which clearly shows you won't put up with being treated like this in the future.

If they laugh off the comment or dismiss your attempt to open a conversation about it, repeat what you said: 'But I was hurt by what you said/ did.' No one should dismiss your feelings, and this should be a strong boundary set so the behaviour isn't repeated in the future.

If they still don't take what you're saying seriously or suggest the hurt is due to your sensitivity instead of their actions, try: 'I understand it might not have been your intention to offend me, but your words/actions did.'

Hopefully this will be enough to elicit an apology and modify the way they talk to you in future. You've drawn a very clear line that they should respect. If you experience something similar in the future, it's much easier to refer back to this conversation. 'Remember when we talked about the way you made me feel when you said/ did xxx? You've done it again by xxx.'

Repetitive behaviour of this kind suggests your friend doesn't respect your boundaries. While hurtful, this is not the kind of person you deserve in your life, so I'd say it's time to call time on the friendship and walk away knowing you gave them a chance, explained their behaviour was hurtful and set a clear boundary.

Before you cut a friend out

Before you make the decision to remove a toxic friend from your life, check in and make sure there's not something bigger going on which is causing them to act out in this way. Surely they weren't like this when you became friends? (If they were and you've just realized it, please feel free to step away now.)

People's behaviour often changes in times of crisis. If they have suddenly started distancing themselves, it could be because of something they are going through rather than something you have done. You are allowed to be hurt but also have to accept we can't control other people and that their actions are not a reflection of your worth.

Open up a dialogue and tell them you are there for them if they are going through something difficult. If they dismiss it out of hand, you have done the right thing by offering support and can walk away without feeling bad about it.

If there is no cause and you tolerate their bad behaviour, you are enabling them. The longer you don't speak up, the more you are signalling that you accept the way in which you are being treated, and the longer it will continue. They might not even be aware that their treatment of you is rude.

The few friendships I have had turn toxic have often been due to their behaviour after drinking alcohol. When you call people out on this, you're often regarded as a bore, uptight, a killjoy, etc. Ultimately, however, if someone's attitude and the way they act upsets you, causes anxiety or ruins your time together, you are entitled to ask them not to drink so much. If they refuse, spend less time with them. You are not responsible for another adult, and if your time together is spoilt by alcohol there is a problem – and it's not yours.

How to deal with a toxic friend

You've had a conversation and explained their behaviour has upset you but you feel the friendship is over – what next?

Limit your contact

Many of us find the idea of ending a friendship dramatic and overwhelming, but you can limit your contact with the person and see if there's a balance you can maintain. If you still care for them, arrange to see them in a group situation with mutual friends. If it's their behaviour while drinking that causes an issue, always leave before the end of the night and make sure you've planned your journey home. For many people, moving a frenemy from your inner friendship circle to an outer one and limiting your time with them is an easier option than cutting them out of your life completely, especially if you have many mutual pals. If this is the best option for you, it doesn't make you weak or a walkover. Just make the decision that feels right to you.

Let it go

If you've had that conversation and/or limited your time with them and your friend is still upsetting you, walk away. You can explain in a letter or message, or have a conversation with them. Tell them that you've become increasingly upset by their attitude towards you, especially when A, B, C happened. Don't bring anyone else into this; it's just between you. Say you wish them well in the future but you have to take a break from the friendship because it's not good for your personal well-being. It might be just the shock they need to take a look at themselves and remedy their behaviour so they get in touch and you can move forward tentatively, but many people may not be able to deal with it. In which case, you are better off without their negativity in your life.

Managing the fallout

If you decide to end a friendship there can be a ripple effect within a friendship group and cutting a person out could be socially risky for you. You will no doubt be questioned about what went wrong by mutual friends. In my experience, explain that the behaviour hurt you and left you with no choice but to walk away. Don't get into a bitching session. Slagging someone off will only reflect badly on you. You may find friends share their own experiences of the person hurting them, or this might be isolated to you. Don't ask friends to take sides. This is your experience and the best thing you can do is walk away and be happy.

Ghosting

Ghosting someone is hurtful, whether it's a friend or within a relationship, but often it's about the other person, not you.

A friend of mine had a girlfriend disappear from her life for no apparent reason. They'd spent the day together, said they'd meet up again soon and then nothing. No texts, no calls, no interaction on social media. Months went past. She felt 'upset, betrayed, angry and shocked. It was as bad as a relationship breakup'. It was the not knowing why and second-guessing herself.

She assumed she'd done something wrong. Three months later her friend reappeared in her life with a text to say that she'd had a bad breakup, things had gone wrong in her life and she'd retreated. An explanation at last but my friend said, 'It was so disrespectful I couldn't forgive her.'

Ultimately, friendship is about communication in good times and bad. If you're going through a rough patch – days, weeks or even months – let your close friends know, even with a text to say, 'Having a hard time at the moment and not up to socializing. I hope you'll understand. Taking some time to regroup and hope we can see each other when I'm back on my feet.'

If someone disappears from your life and you're feeling helpless, upset and confused by their actions, take back control. Write them an old-fashioned pen-and-paper letter explaining that you don't know why they walked away from your friendship but you deserve to be treated better. You wish them well in their lives but anyone who lacks the good manners to explain why they no longer want to spend time with someone they once considered a close friend doesn't deserve your love and energy. Hopefully this will give you the closure you need to move forward.

The Friendship Formula survey...

Have you ever had a friendship turn toxic?

70% Yes
30% No

'She lied to me and slept with my fiancé!'

'I've learnt never to mix business and friendship. It turned out I was being used for free services and as soon as I stopped allowing them to use me for freebies or discounts they badmouthed my business, spread untrue rumours causing loss of clients.'

'Yes, always over a boy – they either slept with or kissed a boy I was interested in!'

'A friend was always belittling me behind my back and the icing on the cake was she had an affair with my now ex-husband.'

'I was gradually frozen out by a group of friends. The worst thing was our children were friends and they froze my daughter out too! Bitches!'

'We were due to go away on holiday together but instead of booking a holiday with me she booked a solo holiday and didn't give me a reason.'

The death of a friend

I met Katie Haines on her birthday, although I didn't know at the time because it was her first day in our office and she didn't mention it until later that day.

On 2 February 2010, Katie wrote on my Facebook wall: 'Just remembered, I started at [magazine] on my birthday so it's my anniversary with you and Karen [our mutual friend] this week!'

That was the kind of woman she was – celebrating our 'friendship anniversaries'.

We met working on a celebrity magazine and quickly became great friends, gossiping about boys and sharing a bottle of wine after work with our mates. Katie left to work on another magazine but she'd soon had enough of celebrities and ended up working as a press officer at the University of Oxford. A 'proper job', we laughed. I was really proud of her.

Despite moving in different social circles and living far apart, we always kept in touch and arranged nights out when we could. I remember going to stay at her house, doing a pub crawl in the town and ending up playing darts in the pub with her boyfriend and mates. Another night, four of us girls went out dancing and ended up doing shots in a nightclub. I fell over. There was drunk karaoke back at her house and hangovers the next day. I'll always be grateful to have taken a lot of questionable photos of us all on that night.

We talked dating, office bitches and career changes, played online Scrabble together, shared an obsession with McDreamy in *Grey's Anatomy* and discussed our dream of writing books… The usual stuff women in their late twenties and early thirties chat about. More fluff than deep and meaningful. The future was bright. We were excited to see what it held for us. Optimistic because we tried to be good people and good things would come our way.

Because Katie really was a good person. Not perfect – no one is – but bloody wonderful. A smile so wide – on a Facebook photo of Katie laughing she commented, 'Good god how big is my mouth?!' I now have that photo framed – a heart so big, laugh so loud and energy that was contagious.

She ran marathons and raised money for charities while I cheered her on from the side moaning about the cold. She travelled with passion and devoured novels with the same appetite as me. We saw each other as much as our busy lives allowed.

Katie married the love of her life, Rich, in a fairy tale winter wedding in December 2009. We jumped around the dance floor with our friend Karen and her other best mates to The Black Eyed Peas' *I Gotta Feeling* and Beyoncé's *Single Ladies*.

When Katie and Rich returned from honeymoon, we arranged a girls' night in with our friends Karen and Helen to celebrate Katie's birthday. I'd love to be able to tell you everything we talked about that night but it's a blur of red wine, cheese and very loud home-karaoke until the wee hours. I do know it was a hilarious evening making plans for the future. My last memory of Katie is standing at the window of the flat watching her get in the car with Helen and waving them off as they drove away.

Two weeks later the phone rang. It was Karen. 'Katie's dead.'

Confused, I asked which Katie. Because it wasn't our Katie. She wasn't sick. But it was. Katie had died the night before on 18 February 2010, her life tragically cut short when she died of carbon monoxide poisoning at home.

I can't begin to describe the devastation Katie's death left behind; and I won't begin to compare my grief to that of her incredible family who I've remained in touch with.

The death of a friend is rarely talked about. When a friend dies, it doesn't feel like you have the 'right' to grieve in the same way you can when a family member dies. Having lost my three grandparents in my late teens and twenties, I had experienced the sadness, loss and tears of grief, but while I still miss my grandparents to this day, losing Katie was, without doubt, the most devastating thing to happen in my life.

Grief is a physical pain. It sucks the air out of your lungs, pokes pins in your heart and twists your guts tight. The unexpected death of a loved one is surreal.

When Katie died, I called work and through sobs said I wouldn't be coming in. Through tears I drove to my friend Karen's flat – where just two weeks before we'd danced around singing and laughing – and sat in absolute shock. We messaged friends who'd worked with Katie so they would hear the news from someone they knew, and watched wide-eyed as Katie's death made the London news, using an old photo of her that we knew she'd be pissed off about.

I don't remember much from the first weeks following Katie's death. You go back to work, but acting 'normal' feels like an insult. People don't know what to say to you, whether to mention your friend or not. You're emotional. Sensitive. Life is surreal. Just being alive feels like a betrayal of kinds.

The funeral was a blur of tears and shock for her friends and family. I've kept in touch with them over the past nine years. We mark Katie's birthday and the anniversary of her death every year. We tag each other in photos and social media posts that bring memories flooding back. In 2019, Katie should have turned forty. A memorial service is taking place, which I know will be both emotional and uplifting.

Grief is there to fill the void left after death. When you lose a friend, you go through the grieving process of shock, anger and heartbreak. A million emotions and nonsensical thoughts. The loss of your future friendship, of what might have been. The guilt of knowing your own grief cannot be compared to that of your friend's family. And yet, it's there.

All these years later, my grief for Katie lingers and occasionally surprises me. Sometimes memories just fill me with joy. A song we sang together makes me smile. I achieve a life goal and think, 'I wonder what Katie would make of this,' while deep down knowing exactly what she'd think. At other times, I'm wracked with sobs. And then I'll realize I've not thought about her for weeks and feel bad.

Katie's death changed me. I think when a

friend dies, a part of your heart dies too. You've tasted a bitterness of life that you never quite recover from. But Katie's death also made me a better person. When I was experiencing an on-going period of unhappiness, one of the things that motivated me to go to therapy was Katie's death – because she doesn't have the gift of life and I should be taking care of myself and making the most of mine. It's not enough to be alive. You have to be living. That's what Katie's death taught me – and I'm thankful to have had that sweet friendship in my life, because the love we shared is worth the pain she left behind.

Sadly, Katie isn't the only friend I miss. My ex-colleague, Gavin Reeve-Daniels, tragically died from pancreatic cancer in September 2014. He was the funniest man I have ever met and I was lucky to sit next to him when we both worked at a celebrity magazine, where he entertained us with jokes and drew comedy sketches. He helped me take myself a little less seriously, put things in perspective and regaled me with stories of his cat and baby son. He left us for a shiny new job and our office was never the same following his departure.

Less than a year later, news broke that Gavin had cancer. Stunned, we sat asking, 'What can we do?' Often in these heartbreaking situations, friends are left wanting to help and feeling useless.

We were determined to show Gavin just how much he was loved. As I already organized charity pub quizzes, I suggested we held one to raise money for a charity of Gavin's choice – Macmillan Cancer Support – and Gav Aid was created. In less than six weeks, a small team, which included Gavin's incredible wife Leesa and journalists who had worked with Gav and adored him, planned a pub quiz which took on a life of its own: two rooms because so many people wanted to come and support Gav, celebrity quiz hosts and DJs, hundreds of quizzers from the world of journalism and PR. Gavin gave the most powerful speech I've ever heard in my life, a battle cry against cancer, and we raised tens of thousands for Macmillan Cancer Support.

Gavin dealt with his terminal diagnosis with grace, dignity and humour. He died suddenly, leaving all who knew him heartbroken. There was anger, sadness and a natural feeling that life just wasn't fair. He was one of the good ones. Cancer really is a bastard.

A year later, Team Gav Aid reformed in Gavin's memory. We got a bigger venue, more celebrity faces, more quizzers. A night tinged with sadness and tears as family members spoke in his place and his battle-cry speech from the year before was shown to a roar of applause. We raised thousands, this time for Pancreatic Cancer Action.

We took our disbelief and anger that Gavin and his family had had to suffer in this way and channelled it into the only positive thing we could think of – raising money and helping others.

Both Katie's and Gavin's deaths left a path of anger, pain, tears and frustration in their wake. Their stories do not belong to me. Both their families have kindly allowed me to share them here – because I couldn't write a book about friendship without thinking about the people who have left an imprint on my heart.

We deal with a tsunami of emotions after the death of someone we love – friend or relative. Grief is, as the famous quote goes, the price we pay for love.

Lessons from grief

This is what my experience of losing a friend taught me about grief.

When a friend dies, you are entitled to your grief. Of course, our bereavement is different to the devastation of their family's, but do not feel guilty for your grief. You may find yourself in a position where you are supporting your friend's family or other friends and not able to express your own grief. Find a mutual friend, or someone who didn't even know them, and talk. And talk some more. Grief is not selfish. And, just like love, I believe it should be shared.

If you're supporting someone who has lost a friend, be patient. Don't shy away from mentioning their name. Check in on them regularly in the weeks and months after. Remind them that they can talk about their friend anytime, and encourage them to share memories. Just listening is really all you need to do.

Be honest with work colleagues in the weeks and months after the death of a friend. Many things can trigger a wave of grief and it's better that your managers and friends at work know that you've suffered a loss so you can excuse yourself and take a moment if you need to. There may also be someone you can talk to at work, so get in touch with HR and see what support there is for you.

Allow yourself to feel sad. You'll no doubt be wracked with guilt for going out partying soon after a loss. I know I was. Grief can make you behave in ways you wouldn't usually do: drink too much; have sex with people you shouldn't; take uncalculated risks. So, while people might want to take you out and 'cheer you up' at some point after your friend's death, one too many drinks can see you sobbing in the corner or unleashing your fury. Ask friends to look after you when you do go out and make sure you get home safely.

There is no timeline for grief. Loss is something you carry forward with you in life, not something you get over. Don't put pressure on yourself.

Grief manifests itself in many ways, impacting on your physical, mental and emotional wellbeing. Looking after every aspect of your health is vital, especially in the early weeks after a loss.

You may not feel like it, but getting outside in the fresh air, taking a walk and simply breathing will do you the world of good. Eat well. Avoid drinking too much. Don't forget, alcohol is a depressant. Don't be embarrassed to seek help if you need to: go and see your doctor, a counsellor or mental health specialist if grief triggers anxiety or depression. You owe it to your friend to take care of yourself in the same way you wish you could take care of them.

If you're feeling lost and frustrated, channel your anger into doing something positive, like raising money for charity. Don't suppress your emotions but do give them an outlet. It helps to find some form of purpose from a loss that makes no sense. In time, you may go days, weeks, even months without thinking about your friend. That's OK, too. It does not make you a bad person. It doesn't mean you didn't love them, and it doesn't mean you are over their death. You are simply living, just as they would want you to. Be kind to yourself and don't beat yourself up.

Memories – and therefore grief – can come out of nowhere and smack you so hard in the face you feel you'll need reconstructive surgery.

I broke down at a rugby sevens tournament in Hong Kong months after Katie's death because they played 'our song' – *I Gotta Feeling* by The Black Eyed Peas – which we'd danced to at her hen weekend and then wedding. When *Grey's Anatomy* played Snow Patrol's *Chasing Cars* during yet another death scene I was a snotty mess. That's Katie's song.

One day you will be able to look back at Facebook memories in your timeline and smile instead of sob. You'll swap stories of drunk nights out with your friend's family. If you can, catch up with your friend's relatives and see mutual friends so you can reminisce, look back and laugh. If you don't see them in person, make the effort to keep in touch on social media – especially your friend's parents, partners and siblings. Their grief is insurmountable and the fact that their loved one is still remembered by friends for years to come will mean a lot.

Live your best life. Pay tribute to your friend by living your life to its fullest. Don't feel guilt for the extra years you're given that they miss, but make the most of them. Make happiness your only goal.

Appreciate your years. When Katie died, I promised myself I'd never complain about ageing. So, while my grey hairs make me roll my eyes, the laughter lines around my eyes multiply each year and my left knee clicks and creaks, I remind myself to be thankful for all the signs of ageing. Growing older is a privilege denied to many wonderful people.

You'll still cry for your friend randomly at times. And that's OK too.

Andy Langford, chief operating officer at Cruse Bereavement Care, says:

'The death of a friend, especially a close friend, can be absolutely devastating. There is no hierarchy in grief, so regardless of whether you are a family member or a friend, the death of a loved one can lead to debilitating sadness and grief and that needs to be recognized. Unfortunately, the death of a friend can be underestimated by society and in the workplace. Under the Employment Rights Act 1996, most employees have the right to take time off work if the person who has died is a dependant. This can mean that your employer might not give you time off after a friend has died, which can be incredibly difficult if you are grieving.

People who are grieving for a friend can assume their grief isn't as important or as serious as the family's, and they can feel guilty for showing their feelings. We all grieve differently and should not feel guilty for how we feel after the death of a loved one; we all deserve the right and space to grieve. The death of a friend can also affect relationships within the wider friendship group. We all experience grief differently and whilst some members of the group may want to regularly meet up and talk, others may feel isolated and alone. It can be difficult to predict and can cause conflict, which is common after a bereavement.

Everyone's grief is unique and there is no right or wrong way to feel after the death of a friend. Take one day at a time and be kind to yourself by eating regularly and getting some rest. You might find talking to someone who knew the friend who has died helpful.

Expressing your feelings through talking or writing can help you to open up about how you are feeling.'

Cruse Bereavement Care say it's important that you take care of yourself following the death of a loved one. Here's their advice:

Do...

+ Talk to other people about the person who has died, about your memories and your feelings.

+ Look after yourself. Eat properly and try to get enough rest (even if you can't sleep).

+ Give yourself time and permission to grieve.

+ Seek help and support if you feel you need it.

+ Tell people what you need.

Don't...

- Isolate yourself.

- Keep your emotions bottled up.

- Think you are weak for needing help.

- Feel guilty if you are struggling to cope.

- Turn to drugs or alcohol – the relief will only be temporary.

The parent trap

There is one thing that I believe is 100 per cent guaranteed to change any friendship: parenthood. It's a subject discussed by all my friends – mums and child-free women like me. The blessing of a baby can create wonderful new bonds and also tear friendships apart. While men may find friendships shift after one or both become a dad, it seems women's friendships are impacted even more.

Let's not assume all family set-ups are the same – I have friends who are same-sex parents, single parents, dads with full-time custody of their kids – but the one thing all mums and dads have in common is a severe lack of free time. Wind back the clock to before that bundle of joy came along and many of you will know that a friendship comes under threat long before the pitter-patter of tiny feet. People often feel cast aside when a friend falls in love and disappears to get to know their new partner.

This isn't an anti-marriage or anti-relationship rant, I promise! But having seen friendships slip away after the exchange of 'I dos', it's time to explore how to maintain friendships when partners and kids come into the picture – because the responsibility lies with both friends.

Love you, bye!

One University of Oxford study found that falling in love can cost you two close friends. Ouch! 'People who are in romantic relationships – instead of having the typical five [individuals] on average, they only have four in that circle. Bearing in mind that one of those is the new person that's come into your life, it means you've had to give up two others,' Robin Dunbar, a professor of evolutionary anthropology, has explained.

This means that, as your inner circle of friends drops from five of the people you are closest to and is now made up of your partner and three others, two close friends are moved into the next circle – and the friendships can naturally deteriorate. 'If you don't see people, your emotional engagement with them drops off and does so quickly,' Professor Dunbar has said. 'The intimacy of a relationship – your emotional engagement with it – correlates very tightly with the frequency of your interactions with those individuals.'

William Rawlins, professor of interpersonal communication at Ohio University, has also found marriage can be the catalyst that ends even the closest of friendships. 'The largest drop-off in friends in the life course occurs when people get married,' he has said. 'And that's kind of ironic, because [at the wedding] people invite both of their sets of friends, so it's kind of this last wonderful and dramatic gathering of both people's friends, but then it drops off.'

It's a sad fact that some friendships simply fade away like a Polaroid photograph, never to be transformed into multicolour again – something to look back on with fond memories and smile, but definitely belonging in the past. No one gets more than twenty-four hours in their day and the needs of family – a partner and children – will undoubtedly take priority over those of friends. When you know you'll be leaving your family short if you fill up friends' glasses first, it's friends who will end up being thirsty for your time.

Changing nappies and changing friendships

Sometimes it feels like I've been standing at the top of the parenting path for the past decade clinging onto my gin and tonic with an inane grin on my face, waving to my friends as they skip off together into the sunset, pushing their Bugaboos with glee while swapping weaning tips.

Friends brush past me – men with their mini-mes tucked into a papoose, women who have had baby number two in their early forties – to gather in the play park. I've watched for over fifteen years, so now many of my mates have teenagers, tweenagers, toddlers and teething tots – biological, adopted, surrogate, how these beautiful children got here is irrelevant. Some are with partners, some are alone. All are families.

I was recently asked by someone I'd just met, 'Do you have a family?' I knew exactly what she meant. A family of my own. But I wasn't sure how to answer, so I replied, 'I have a mum, dad and sister but if you mean my own… no.' There are many reasons a person doesn't have children. If a man or woman doesn't, any conversation should be approached with caution. Quite frankly, just don't even ask, because it's none of your damn business. For some it is a choice, for others it's not. Either way, the crack that is created between friends when babies come along can become as wide as the Grand Canyon if you BOTH don't throw in some time and love.

Priorities change. That's a given. Becoming a parent is all-consuming, and friendships are the first thing to be shelved, to collect a fine layer of dust until mum – or dad – are ready to put their child down, pick up their friend, dust them off and try to re-establish the friendship.

New mums can struggle with feelings of isolation, depression and a loss of identity. Childless women can face insensitive questions and assumptions about why their wombs have remained vacant. There is so much sensitivity surrounding motherhood – the decision to have a child, the surprise unplanned pregnancy, the yearning for a baby when you don't have a partner, infertility issues, the loss of a child, and so much more. It's no wonder women's friendships can become fractured when baby talk begins. I've seen resentment build between mums and non-mums. Children bring so much to our lives but they make everything a lot more complicated, right?

I've also been given the gift of other people's children in my life. Being an aunt, godmother and honorary auntie is one of my most fulfilling and proudest achievements. Of course, these kids have transformed the friendships I have with their parents, but if the relationship was based on love and understanding rather than cocktails and gossip, it's much easier to go the distance. You adapt. Take a crash course in mum-talk. Support your mate through the ups and downs of motherhood – because, ultimately, mums are all rock stars with a mini-entourage. My advice to non-mums – join in, because it's a hell of a ride!

Life and confidence coach – and mum of two – Charlie O'Brien says...

'When babies arrive on the scene inevitably friendships change, especially if one of you has children and the other doesn't. But it absolutely doesn't need to be the end...

Childfree...

If you're the friend without children it may feel like the woman you've loved, confided in and got horrendously drunk with for years has been lost to a savage sea of nappies, vomit and baby talk. And you're partly right. Your friend has gone through the biggest life shift there is. She has been reborn as a mother. Her baby is the centre of her universe and quite rightly so – but underneath the pile of baby washing she's still the same woman she always was. And chances are she's desperate for adult conversation, a night out and a G&T!

Lunches, coffees and evenings out will take more forward planning than they used to, but you can be a helping hand. Ask if you can come round and watch the baby while she has a bath and gets ready. She will appreciate it more than you'll know. And the best friendships thrive when you take an active interest in each other's lives. So get to know the baby, be part of their family life, listen to her moan. Embrace this new chapter with her and, remember, she's still the same woman you love.

Mums...

If you're the one consumed with breastfeeding, baby-grows and sleep schedules it's important you don't forget your child-free friends. Motherhood is all-consuming, especially in those early sleepless days, but there is nothing more refreshing than FaceTiming your best mate and chatting about something non-baby related. Keep your bond strong by taking an interest in her accomplishments, achievements and, of course, her stresses. Women without children can often feel sidelined as everyone around them starts families. It can be a lonely time.

Remind your friend that, even though it may be a while until you feel up to a night out again, she's always welcome at yours for a takeaway and a catch-up. All relationships take work and compromise especially through periods of change, and it's great to remind yourself about why you became friends in the first place.

Becoming a mum doesn't mean you only need 'mum friends'. In fact, it's wonderful to stay close to those who knew you BEFORE you had children. They will help you hang on to your identity outside of motherhood. Sometimes relationships end; people change and friendships drift apart – and that's OK too. A friendship takes work and love on both sides and, if one party stops doing that, it may be time to move on.'

My guide to helping friendship survive motherhood

Mums...

When you have children, the freedom you once enjoyed all but disappears; your friendships will adapt, change and some will fall by the wayside.

When your free time is limited, you're allowed to be fussy about who you spend it with, so it's only natural you'll concentrate on your inner circle and let some friends go. Do it guilt-free. The best people will keep in touch, check in on you, ask if you need help and be there to take you out for the night when you feel ready to leave baby at home for the first time.

As a parent you have to put your child's needs – AND your own – first. That can be hard for any friend to accept, but if they are not willing to adapt and come along for the ride, they can't offer what you need in a friend anyway. Send us photos of your kids, tell us their funny stories, make us part of their lives, and don't be afraid to reveal your parenting fails too. You are our window into motherhood. But NEVER utter, 'You won't understand because you're not a mum.'

Try to put aside a day or weekend, even just once a year, to spend with your best friends without your children. We know it's a big ask, but when you give us your full attention (phones away please) it feels like we have our old friend back. Investing time in your closest friends will pay off in the long run too – who do you think will be there to babysit/do emergency school pick-ups/be there for your teenager to confide in/spoil your kids rotten?

Non-mums...

You have to get used to half-listened-to conversations when there's a baby about, and when your friend gets up and walks away in the middle of a deep and meaningful chat to tend to their kid you bite your tongue. They also forget what you were talking about and seem distracted, mostly because sleep deprivation is a form of torture they suffer every night at the lungs of their little one. Don't take it personally. Accepting your new place in your friend's life takes time, but if your friendship runs deep, invest time with your mum friend now and you'll create a whole new role in her life and the baby's.

Planning is everything. There are no impromptu get-togethers. There will often be a start and finish time to any social event revolving around naps/feeding/bath/relieving the babysitter. Get used to it. Diarize, make the most of the time you have together *sans* kids, and embrace the madness of spending time with your friends' kids too. It's a real honour to be part of a child's life and the bond you build with them is really special.

Mums speak in another language, which they became fluent in seemingly overnight in the maternity ward: Mum-glish. New words and phrases are introduced: mastitis (instead of Merlot), sleep training (not gym training) and NCT (nothing to do with SJP). Make the effort to learn so she can talk to you in her hour of need. There will be new 'mum friends' around, but don't assume she feels comfortable discussing everything with them.

Be patient. You'll miss the life you had with your friend before babies, but don't wallow – embrace the change, throw yourself into your auntie role and have fun. Friends' kids are a great excuse to be a big kid yourself – I have far too much fun with face paints, rollercoasters, zombie stories, teen movies, hide-and-seek, laser tag and *Baby Shark* than is probably decent for a child-free woman of my age! And I love it.

Dear mums,

a letter from your non-mum friends...

I love you. And I love your child. But things have really changed between us since you became a mother. The joy you have in your life makes me happy, but I miss the old us too.

I want to be part of your life but can't help feeling rejected. You don't have time for me like before. I get it.

I'm supposed to be a grown-up about this, and understanding, but sometimes I just feel you slipping away from me.

I miss our nights out. And gossiping for hours. Comparing hangovers and dating disasters.

Our lives are so different now, and they'll never be the same again. I'm not a priority. And sometimes that hurts. Then I feel guilty for being selfish. Because I'm happy you're happy. Honestly, I am.

I like spending time with your kids – they are hilarious – but I'd like more time with you just by myself, to discover what we still have in common as two friends. But I'm scared that we'll realize we don't have much in common now after all.

So I'll be patient. I'll learn all about Iggle Piggle and homemade slime. I'll make sure I always remember your kids' birthdays. I'll sympathize when you're exhausted and not compare it to when I'm knackered from a night out. I'll listen to your mum worries and try to sympathize.

I promise to be here when you want to talk. But let's make sure it's not just about mum stuff. I'll try not to be jealous of all your new mum friends that you have loads more in common with than me now.

I want you to know I love you. And I'm so proud of the mum and woman you are.

Jo Wimble-Groves, aka mum blogger Guilty Mother, says...

'When I met my husband, he was already aware of how important my friends were to me and he accepted that he would have to share me.

I consider myself lucky to have had the same best friend since I was twelve years old. She hugged and scooped me up when my parents divorced in the most unamicable way and I was the one who had to move out. In our twenties, we supported each other over disastrous boyfriends. It was always our relationship that remained the most stable.

During our three decades of friendship, we have seen each other at our best and at our worst. We've weathered storms together and seen both our husbands become terribly unwell and supported each other as they both recovered (to a degree). We watched each other have children and I was one of the first to hold her third baby in the hospital.

As we became parents, the juggling act really started to crank up a notch. These busy, full-on days mean that we often go weeks or even months without seeing each other. My advice? If they are the most loyal of friends to you, then when you see them, it should feel like you have never been apart. If you have at least one friendship like that, make sure you hold on to it tight.'

The Friendship Formula survey...

Have you lost a friend when they became a parent?

45% Yes
55% No

'When I had kids, a close friend didn't contact me. Another ghosted me. They were both undergoing IVF.'

'I've resented the changes a baby brings to a friendship, particularly as I suffer from infertility and have been going through treatment.'

'I've struggled with friends having kids but only because I have been so desperate to have my own.'

'I miss my friends when I don't see them as much, but I don't resent them or anyone.'

'Give it time – people come back once they are no longer drowning in parenthood.'

'Roll with it. Embrace it. Become a part of the

family. Those children will keep your friendship going for far longer. Because they'll keep asking to see you too.'

'Accept that the friendship changes more for them than you. Don't assume they can't come out. Keep inviting them but have realistic expectations.'

11

Just good friends

Just good friends?

The age-old question: can men and women just be good friends? Did they even manage to answer it properly in 1989's *When Harry Met Sally*?

In my teens, my closest friend was actually my mate Ian who I met when I was about fifteen. He's been a constant in my life ever since, and although we don't see each other as much as we'd like, I know he's always there for me.

Going to an all-girls school meant I lacked male friendship until I changed school for my A levels. There were boys around, and my attitude to friendships between the genders changed.

For the first time in my life I had a group of guy friends who I was close to. The only rule to being one of the lads was I couldn't snog any of them (or rather, they couldn't snog me). However, some of those boys liked to complicate things… Which led me to question whether men and women can really just be good friends. It seemed there was always an attraction on one side or the other.

Anyway, these guys taught me that it's possible to be friends with members of the opposite sex without snogging getting in the way – and I'm still friends with many of them to this day. They showed me the special bond between guys and the difference between women's friendships and men's.

Here's what I learnt about being friends with boys:

- Men don't hold grudges the way women do. They are quicker to let disagreements go.

- Sometimes we don't see each other or speak for years, but the expectation that the friendship hasn't faltered is still there. We just pick it up where we left off.

- They don't over-analyze what you say. My male friends take things on face value and never expect to read between the lines of what I'm saying.

- There's no point being subtle or dropping hints. Just get to the point and don't expect them to be a mind reader.

Friendship between men and women is a fairly recent phenomenon. For hundreds of years women only spent time with male relatives, potential suitors and then their husband. The idea that straight men and women could be friends and nothing more was questionable until more recent decades.

When I was younger there were complicated platonic friendships, but in my adult years I've had some fantastic friendships with men with no hint of sexual tension. I've had other great friendships with guys I've fancied but never told. I've also asked out guy friends believing there was more to their attention only to be directed to the 'friend zone' for my efforts. Gutted at the time, I later realized it was their loss. But if you think it's possible for men and women to be 'just good friends' – in the sense that there is zero sexual attraction felt by either party – you're in the minority.

A 2012 study at the University of Wisconsin showed that it's impossible to escape from sexual tension. Scientists studied 88 opposite-sex friend couples and found that men were more physically and sexually attracted to their female friends than the women were to the guys. The study found that these men were also more likely to overestimate how attracted their platonic female friends were to them, while the women underestimated how attractive they were to their male friends. Basically, the men assumed the women were secretly attracted to them and the women assumed the men weren't interested in them sexually. The men and women who said they had no physical or sexual attraction to their friend were in significantly longer friendships when compared to those who felt an attraction.

We can blame evolution for the base belief that men and women can't be 'just good friends'.

According to lead researcher, April Bleske-Rechek, men tend to be more attracted to their female friends because they face the risk of being genetically 'shut out' if they don't take 'advantage of various reproductive opportunities'.

All friendship is based on a chemistry of sorts, so it's easy to see how this can develop into sexual attraction. There will always be some of us who struggle to be platonic with friends – particularly men with female pals if the study is anything to go by.

Back in 2000, a study published in the *Journal of Social and Personal Relationships* reported that out of more than 300 college students, 67 per cent had had sex with a friend. However, 56 per cent of these friendships decided not to take it to a romantic level after the encounter – they clearly valued their friendship over sex.

A 2017 survey of 6,500 people commissioned by social network MeetMe found more than half had fantasized about sleeping with their best friend of the opposite gender. Nearly 40 per cent had actually slept with said best friend – and two-thirds admitted they would if the opportunity presented itself!

What I've learnt about being friends with heterosexual men over the years is that they offer something different and unique compared to my friendships with women and gay guys. My straight male mates offer up a varying perspective on relationships, offer solutions to problems, always make me feel valued and treat me as an absolute equal. While our conversation differs wildly from those with the women in my life, I've been surprised by just how similar men and women actually are. I've sat with some of my closest guy friends as they've shared fertility issues, marriage breakup stories, honest views on being a father and grief.

I think the biggest difference in these friendships is the emotional attachment and commitment. I don't expect the same level of understanding and support from men as I do women. There's a deeper level of understanding from women, simply because they are more likely to have walked a mile in my size 5s. According to author Ronald Riggio, research shows that men bond over activities, like sporting events and travel, while women are more likely to share emotions and talk about feelings.

What makes friendships between women arguably closer than those of different genders is that emotional bond – but emotions run high and can also be the cause of conflict and fallouts. Platonic friendship between different genders offers a similar closeness but without the heightened emotional attachment and high expectation of investment from the other person. My male friends seem to be more laid-back in their approach, more casual in locking in plans and chilled if you have to rearrange them. I know this isn't because they don't care, they just don't feel the need to overstate something; just by wanting to hang out with you they feel they are communicating – they just don't feel the need to make declarations of their (platonic) feelings for you. In my experience, men show you they care about you just by spending time with you. They don't need to reinforce this with words or big gestures.

I go to England rugby matches with a girlfriend, to the theatre and on holiday with a mixed-gender group. I talk emotions and relationship hopes and dreams with guys as well as girls. So, rather than making sweeping generalizations, I'd preach we should discard the gender stereotypes of friendship and be friends simply because of who the person is and what they bring to your life in conversation, acts of kindness and fun.

Perhaps men's relationships have evolved. I've certainly witnessed the closeness between men I know supporting each other when dealing with a health crisis or death of a parent in exactly the same way a woman would. Ultimately, if you're a good person, your reproductive organs are not going to dictate the kind of friend you are.

Sex and relationship expert Annabelle Knight says...

'We can definitely transcend our animal brains and be friends with members of the opposite sex. For one, we're not attracted to every single potential partner out there and the longer you know a person in a specific context, in this case as a friend, the less likely you are to want to try and turn that friendship into something romantic. It's within us to preserve our friendships, so doing anything that may endanger them is usually something we tend to avoid. Having a friend of the opposite sex can be hugely beneficial to you; they can provide a different take on life, one that you might not get from friends of the same sex.'

The Friendship Formula survey...

Do you believe men and women can be 'just good friends'?

80% Yes
20% No

'Of course you can just be good friends. I am bisexual so I have to believe this otherwise I'd have no friendships. Sex doesn't have to complicate everything.'

'I've been friends with two guys since nursery and we've never been anything other than friends.'

'I feel some kind of sexual chemistry always

gets in the way. I think people have a much stronger bond with friends of the same gender as them.'

'I have had and do have male friends where I believe there are no feelings. We have fun together, can provide advice that someone of the same sex can't and the sex thing doesn't have to get in the way.'

'As a man it's so important to have female input into your life. I have a whole load of female friends and instead of a best man I had a best woman at my wedding.'

Friends with benefits

So you're just good friends... and there's an attraction. Maybe an alcohol-fuelled flirtation. You end up sleeping together – and decide to keep having sex but just as friends. Are friends with benefits a good idea or is a fallout inevitable?

One study in 2005 by Mikayla Hughes, Kelly

Morrison and Kelli Jean K. Asada identified the motivation for people to seek friends-with-benefits (FWB) relationships: relationship avoidance, sex, relationship simplicity and emotional connection. There are many advantages to a FWB agreement. You can enjoy sex without romantic complications but within the safety and trust of a friendship. A step up from casual sex, many people enjoy the ease of a FWB arrangement, and on paper it seems like the ideal set-up – there's an attraction but not enough to develop into a romance, you don't want to commit to a relationship or you may have come out of something long-term and are looking for something less intense.

A FWB relationship often fizzles out when one or both people meet someone they have a romantic connection with and decide to be in a committed relationship instead, leaving the friendship side of things intact. Of course, there are rules to FWB. If one of you is more emotionally invested than the other or develops feelings, things can get very complicated and the friendship can come crashing down – so communication and honesty is key.

There's always the possibility that FWB turns into something more serious. Look at Mila Kunis and Ashton Kutcher, who ironically both starred in movies about this very kind of friendship arrangement: Mila in *Friends with Benefits* (2011) and Ashton in *No Strings Attached* (2011). The pair started out as friends after meeting on the set of *That '70s Show* in the late 1990s. Mila was only fourteen, Ashton was nineteen. Many years and a few relationships later they started adding benefits to their friendship.

'We were in similar movies and we should have paid attention to them because this doesn't work in real life. We clearly didn't pay attention and we shook hands on it and said we would just have fun. We literally lived out our movies,' Mila has said in an interview. 'He had just got out of a marriage and I had gotten out of a relationship. But we were in agreement that it was just fun. And three months later, I was like, "This isn't just fun anymore." And then a year later we wanted to get married. I think it took everyone by surprise.'

While moving from FWB to a relationship is rare, it isn't impossible. Have fun, stay fun and just be honest!

Sex and relationship expert Annabelle Knight says...

'When it comes to "Friends with benefits", it will only work if you're on the same page. It may seem like a great idea on the surface, but usually the situation works better for one partner than the other. It's almost inevitable that some sort of feelings will develop for one of you. This can cause all sorts of problems surrounding jealousy, a sense of ownership, or that you're owed a certain level of exclusivity. Proceed with caution!'

The Friendship Formula survey...

Have you ever had a friend with benefits?

48% Yes
52% No

'Yes, it didn't end badly, we just went separate ways.'

'During my single days there were always some friends you could turn to if desire struck!'

'We both moved on with partners and the benefits ended there.'

'I ended up having stronger feelings than I planned for him and he's now my fiancé!'

'We enjoyed benefits for a while and then stayed friends but moved on with our personal lives.'

'It was a short-term thing, to fulfil our needs in a safe manner. We've met other people and are still friends.'

The ex files

A quick note about staying friends with exes, as this seems one of the most divisive topics.

For many, the idea is hell. Personally, I think it all depends on the ex and what level of friendship you take away from a breakup. I've remained friends with most of my exes, at least on a basic level of Facebook and the odd text. I've also been to the weddings of ex-lovers, happy to see them married to the love of their life. Yes, it was slightly awkward making small talk with an ex's parents, and there was a cringe moment when a groom's best friend proceeded to inspect my empty ring finger, only to be shown my middle one instead.

I don't think there's one rule for staying mates with a past love. If you still care for each other, and new partners don't have a problem with it, then keeping in touch and meeting up is lovely.

Sex and relationship expert Annabelle Knight says...

'Staying friends with your ex is totally possible, and completely healthy, if you're both firmly on the same page. No, not even that, you have to be same line, same word. If one of you has residual feelings then it just won't work.'

The Friendship Formula survey...

Can you stay friends with an ex?

32% Yes
18% No
50% Depends on the ex

'I don't think it is important but if you ended mutually as just friends and enjoy their company then it's the same as any other friend. I do think this is much easier as you get older however!'

'Yes, because I love them as a person and would miss them being in my life. I just don't fancy them!'

'They are part of your history and if it ended on good terms then why not remain friends? You obviously had a connection to begin with and it would be a shame to lose it if things ended ok.'

'He's not 'in my life' but we are in touch because we dated for a long time and had a mutual break up.'

'My past relationships have always been too intense to just be friends.'

'I don't think it is important that they are still in your life. Just makes things less awkward when you bump into them.'

'Sadly, I haven't managed this due to new partners not being comfortable with me being friends with my ex.'

'Yes, we're friends because ultimately they were a great friend – not a great boyfriend!'

12

Social media mates and meeting IRL

Pokes. Likes. DMs. RTs. Shares. There's a whole other language on social media with a bunch of strangers who are online friends and potentially friends IRL (in real life) too.

I was an early adopter of Friends Reunited (remember the thrill of a school pal finding you while avoiding others?!), Myspace, Facebook, Twitter and Instagram. I loved being able to communicate with friends around the world online. In fact, I ended up incorporating it into my job, and the digital world later became my career. Funny how things turn out, right?

Since the launch of Facebook in 2004, more than a billion people have created Facebook accounts. Americans spend about 56 billion minutes on the site each month! There are many glorious things about social media – but I want to flag some of the more dangerous things, too.

Digital platforms can be full of infighting and smoke and mirrors, projecting images of a perfect Insta life. An online life is not somewhere you should live but simply visit, while remembering it's somewhat of a wonderland. Have fun, use it to support good causes, spread positive messages and bond with like-minded people – but beware the trolls and negativity, and don't be drawn into comparing your real life to other people's online profiles, which are often heavily edited and filtered.

We've looked at friendship circles in Chapter 4, but of course those don't include your social networks. Professor Robin Dunbar from the University of Oxford admits digital platforms can increase the total number of friends we can have at the same time. His studies show that the maximum number of friends it is realistically possible to engage with is about 150, while on social media such as Facebook people will typically have 120–130 friends. Social media has changed the way we interact with people. 'What Facebook does and why it's been so successful in so many ways is it allows you to keep track of people who would otherwise effectively disappear,' Professor Dunbar explains. A 2015 study by Adriana M. Manago, a psychology professor at the University of California, found that millennials have a wider network but their feelings of fulfilment from these interactions are heavily based on shallow connections and public perception.

Lurking – reading posts on social media and watching what people are doing without engaging or posting yourself – isn't particularly good for your well-being or mental health. If you only spend time on social media to gather information about people's lives and compare them to your own, you're going to come away feeling bad about yourself. Facebook – or Facebrag in the case of many people – only offers a glimpse into your friends' lives, while Instagram images are often heavily filtered.

Research suggests that social media can lead people to think that their peers are doing better socially than they are. The 2017 study found social media posts are predominantly focused on projecting the most positive versions of ourselves. Well, of course! The digital world is seen as a benchmark to compare our lives with others, and often the fallout of that is a feeling of failure, envy and FOMO (fear of missing out).

However, having a huge group of online friends can result in 'friendship lite', according to social psychologist Sherry Turkle – meaning we can have lots of surface connections but a lack of deep and meaningful friendships in real life. It's important to cherish those friends we have in our real lives and be fully present while in their company rather than distracted by social media.

Remember:

◆ Just because you're having a good time doesn't mean you have to document it to the world.

◆ Take photos and videos at an event but save the posting until after, so you can fully enjoy your time with friends rather than worrying about which hashtag to use.

◆ Put your phone away during meals. OK, you can take a photo of your food if you have to, but then it goes straight in your bag!

◆ Remind yourself that you're seeing the best bits of someone's life on social media while living the reality of your own. They are not comparable.

◆ Keep an eye on how much time you spend on social media compared to time spent with your friends either in person or on the phone. If you realize you're online more, cut back and make more effort to catch up with your real friends – and enjoy that hug!

I'll admit, there are people on my Facebook that I probably should unfriend because their status updates annoy me (hello friend!), but it's easier to roll my eyes if they come up in the feed and keep scrolling than hit that 'unfriend' button and face questions by people we mutually know. And don't forget to say a little prayer to the algorithm gods that their status updates don't show up in your feed!

If you're very frustrated but can't face the social taboo of blocking someone, you can simply mute them so they never pop up in your feed (and even mute them on Facebook Messenger too). Word of warning: this can make for awkward encounters if they share big life news you miss because they are muted, but you can always blame those algorithm gods and act incredulous that you missed such an important post.

I'm thankful to Facebook for keeping me connected with close friends scattered across the globe. And Twitter for having interesting interactions with people I would never meet in person. And Instagram for introducing me to positive role models and inspirational women. But never forget how important meeting up with friends in real life can be for our well-being. There might be all the feels online but there are no hugs available on the internet.

'We underestimate how important touch is in the social world,' Professor Dunbar has said.

'Words are easy. But the way someone touches you, even casually, tells you more about what they're thinking of you.'

But what happens when you hit it off online and want to move from virtual to real life?

From online to real life

Keep your expectations realistic. Just because you find each other hilarious in 280 characters or fewer doesn't mean you'll be LOLing in person; but if they're your type on screen, the chances are they'll be 'one of your people' in the flesh.

Social media is a great way to connect with like-minded people who you have plenty in common with. Whether it's a romantic or mate date, however, always meet somewhere public. You also don't have to swap numbers – just arrange the details in your DMs and wait until you trust the person to exchange any personal information.

I've met a few people after chatting on social media, with mixed results. One was a girl who offered to show my friend and me around and go for a drink while we were visiting Bangkok for the first time. We agreed to meet for one cocktail and ended up staying out until the early hours of the morning in one of the city's most questionable establishments! She now lives back in the UK but hundreds of miles away, so we haven't had the chance to meet up again, but we keep in touch – on social media! – and I know we'd enjoy another night out in real life together.

Another social media-to-IRL meeting didn't go so well. We had a huge amount in common and I was excited to meet her. We talked for a few hours over wine and bumped into a friend of mine who joined the conversation. All went well, although she was very interested in talking about race issues with my mate, who is black. It wasn't until the following day I found out she'd horrifically offended my friend with some blatant racism when I'd gone to the loo. To say I was mortified is an understatement. You see, you just don't know someone until you spend time with them in person.

Needless to say, when she followed up to meet again, I explained that wouldn't be happening, called her out on insulting my friend and suggested she read some relevant books, like *Why*

I'm No Longer Talking to White People About Race. She apologized, but I don't need or want people like that in my life. My real friends don't deserve that shit in their lives and I feel terrible that the incident happened on my watch.

So, there's the good, the bad and the ugly.

The Friendship Formula Survey...

Have you ever met someone on social media and they have become friends in real life?

'We got chatting about a common interest, ending up attending similar events, and now keep in touch.'

'Yes, I met my friend on Twitter and we met when I went to London. We liked a lot of the same things and I now count her as one of my best friends.'

'I've got a few social media friends who are now real life friends as we live locally and met up at a group social. We've been friends for 10 years.'

'Yes – a mummy blogger on Instagram.'

'I started travelling by myself. I went to Australia and Costa Rica as soon as *Mean Girls* was over. I'm pretty spontaneous so I didn't really know what I was doing. I was terrified and lonely. You see incredible things and there was no-one to share them with. But I think it gave me a bit of chutzpah and ended up being one of the best things I've ever done. It taught me I could survive on very little too. I would do it that way all over again, it was life-changing. You get to prove to yourself, what you're made of.'

Rachel McAdams

13

Loneliness and choosing to be alone

There's a big difference between being alone and feeling lonely. We're going to look at both. You can have a mobile phone full of numbers or be stood in the middle of a party and still feel lonely. There have definitely been periods of my life when I've felt this way, which will probably come as a surprise to my friends. You can be outgoing and seemingly happy but still be very lonely and end up isolating yourself from others as a result – which doesn't help at all! Often when I've felt lonely and neglected, it's simply because the people in my life assumed I was busy. It's your responsibility to reach out to people and let them know when you need company or help.

In 2017, charities Relate and Relationships Scotland released a report called 'You're Not Alone', looking at social relationships in the UK. It was found that almost 7 million adults in the UK say they have no close friends, an increase from one in ten as was the case in 2014–15. The study also found that 45 per cent of UK adults say they feel lonely at least some of the time; almost a fifth said that they feel lonely often or all of the time; and, sadly, around one in six (17 per cent) said they never or rarely feel loved.

While loneliness is often associated with the elderly, it's actually younger people who are more likely to feel lonely. Almost two-thirds of 16–24-year-olds said they feel lonely at least some of the time, and almost a third (32 per cent) feel lonely often or all the time. In 2018, MP Tracey Crouch was appointed what some have dubbed the 'minister for loneliness' to try to tackle the issue of loneliness in the UK. The same year, a study commissioned by the British Red Cross in partnership with the Co-op revealed 9 million people in the UK say they are always or often lonely.

'Loneliness is a major social, educational, economic and health issue that will reach epidemic proportions by 2030,' says Professor Stephen Houghton of the University of Western Australia. It could also be putting your health at risk. Researchers at Brigham Young University in Utah found that loneliness can increase the risk of early death by at least 30 per cent.

According to Katie Leaver, author of *The Friendship Cure*, we need to recognize loneliness and take action. 'When you find the courage to admit that you are lonely, you claim a little control back for yourself. It is not shameful to be lonely – it is human and it is natural and it is salvageable,' Katie says. 'Loneliness is not necessarily the same thing as social isolation. Perhaps the cruellest thing about loneliness is that it can exist in the company of others.'

Back in 2000, Robert D. Putnam published *Bowling Alone: The Collapse and Revival of American Community*, which looked at the disengagement from friends, family, neighbours and community in the US. During nearly 500,000 interviews over twenty-five years, he discovered we belong to fewer clubs, get together with friends less often, spend less time with family and know fewer of our neighbours. Modern life – technology, changes in careers, a varied structure of families – has seen a deterioration in our relationships, which has had a significant impact on our health and well-being. Sad, right?

Social isolation is becoming more common: friends may move away; your job might mean you moving far away from family; divorce can cause emotional and physical upheaval; while many more people work from home too. And, just like happiness, loneliness is contagious. A 2009 study using data collected from roughly 5,000 people and their children found that participants are 52 per cent more likely to be lonely if someone they're directly connected to is lonely.

So what can you do about it if you're feeling lonely?

♦ If you feel lonely because you don't have close friends, start small and challenge yourself to speak to three people every day. They could be in a shop, library, your place of work or the bus stop. Once you get used to making chit-chat, you'll be more confident about joining groups and clubs and starting conversations with potential new friends.

♦ Be aware that loneliness can lead to depression and other mental health issues. This is something you should discuss with your GP.

♦ Don't rely on the internet to be your friend. The 1975's song *The Man Who Married a Robot* springs to mind. While I'm a big fan of social media, it's more important to spend time with people in the real world. Use the internet to enhance your life but don't let it take over.

♦ Don't keep it to yourself. When we feel lonely, it's easy to sit in that loneliness – while others don't even realize we feel this way. Confide in a friend that you are struggling and ask for help or suggestions of things you can do together and with other people.

- Look for ways to meet new people (See Chapter 3). Whether it's volunteering for a local charity, visiting people in hospital or a home, or joining a local club, there are many ways to spend time with people and get to know them.

- Find friends through your passions – join a local book club, ramblers, fitness class at the gym, sign up for an art course or night school. You're guaranteed to have something to discuss and make small talk about.

- Ask friends if they know people who would like to join you when you get together for dinner, a trip to the cinema or the theatre, or a walk. Work towards expanding your social circle through the people you know so you already have someone in common and are more likely to share the same interests.

◆ If you work, see if the company has any clubs you can join. Often there are choirs, etc.

If loneliness is really impacting your life, there are associations and helplines on page 188.

Choosing to be alone

I've lived on my own for fifteen years, and I love it. I've always been very sociable, and during my twenties and early thirties I was out with friends most nights. As I've got older I've spent more and more time alone – sometimes by choice, other times because I've not communicated my needs to friends and family, and occasionally because I'm experiencing anxiety. Mostly, though, being alone in my flat is safe, cosy and a choice.

Throughout my life I've found myself on the periphery of friendship groups, rarely in the middle. I know I have a tendency to join in with activities rather than be the organizer. It's something I'm still trying to figure out myself – how I often don't feel I truly belong, even with people I know care for and love me.

I've also come to realize that I prefer to spend time with friends one-on-one, or in small groups, rather than big gatherings. I shed my social butterfly wings in my twenties and instead love a proper catch-up with people. I often come away from big parties feeling frustrated that I didn't get to have proper conversations with people. It can feel shallow and superficial to me. This could just be a sign of getting older!

When it comes to travel, I've always been on holiday with at least one friend, a group of mates or flown to meet people at the destination. The few days I've been left to my own devices abroad have been marred by anxiety and loneliness. I just didn't particularly enjoy spending time alone on holiday. I took myself to a UK spa hotel for a long weekend – a writing break – and while it was relaxing and I was happy to eat alone, I couldn't destress and enjoy myself. I talked myself through the weekend rather than switching off my inner critic and just enjoying it.

In 2018, while writing this book, I decided I was going to do just that. I wanted to put kindfulness into practice and take myself on a self-care holiday – to step out of my comfort zone and challenge myself, while showing myself some serious self-love. And while it would have been fun to have a girlfriend along for the ride, I decided this was something I had to do alone.

I decided to kick off 2019 in style and booked a flight to Bali on 1 January 2019. When I arrived at the airport, albeit hungover from the night before, the fact I wouldn't know anyone for the next twelve days kicked in. What if I didn't like being alone on the other side of the world? What if I was anxious and felt trapped? What if I got seriously bored of my own company? Thankfully, it was an expensive experiment that paid off.

I spent the first three nights at a hotel in Seminyak. Armed with a travel guide, I set out to explore the town during the day, enjoyed a smoothie in a bar overlooking the beach, wandered around the shops and had the most delicious lunch while people-watching. No one looked at me like I had two heads – or if they did, I didn't notice.

I wasn't nervous, I was excited. This was a very different feeling.

The next couple of days were spent reading and relaxing, getting dressed up and taking myself out for dinner at night. I requested a table for one with no hesitation or embarrassment. I was on a solo adventure and proud of it. It gave me the confidence to realize that most people are so consumed with themselves, they don't give anyone else much attention. Yes, my mobile phone and Wi-Fi were a perfect distraction to kill time, but I tried to spend the days taking in my surroundings and just being in the moment instead of losing myself in a digital world.

After a few days, I headed to Bliss Sanctuary For Women in Canggu for the next week. With only six women staying there at one time, it promised a wellness retreat focused on relaxation and self-care. I'd just got used to my own company when I would be living with strangers for a week. What if we had nothing in common? How would I deal with either making small talk for seven days or isolating myself from the group? I was apprehensive.

What followed was a week of life lessons,

indulging in solitude and reading, early morning yoga, solo sightseeing trips for meditation at the Pyramids of Chi and exploring rice fields; shared meals with strangers who became friends. We were all there for different reasons but mostly to find our sense of self. Some of us were travelling solo for the first time and were amused to find ourselves alone but together. We shared very personal stories and experiences. There were tears. There was a real sense of belonging, and some of us bonded quickly and have kept in touch.

I discovered I like being alone even more than I thought I would, but also relish the company of others. Being alone doesn't mean you're lonely. Learning to spend time on your own is a skill that everyone should master. Moments of solitude with nothing but your thoughts can tap into who you are, who you want to become and how you're going to get there. There is something very centring about stripping back life and living in the present, even for a short time. It was truly one of the most blissful weeks of my life – it taught me so much about who I am and reinforced the way in which I'd like to live my life.

On my return – late due to a case of Bali belly,

emergency doctor, drip and postponed flight! – people said I was brave to travel alone because they'd be too nervous. It's not 'brave' but it has its challenges. Choosing to be alone is empowering. Solo travel is an adventure I'd recommend to anyone. It's the perfect way to be positively selfish – no compromising on the sightseeing schedule, no debating where to eat or what time to head home after a night out. You make up your own rules and then break them if you want with no consequences.

I can't wait to travel with friends again and make some memories together – girls' weekends, adventures with my friend Nick, city breaks with my sister – but am already planning another solo trip to make memories just for me, too.

Remember...

◆ If you're feeling lonely, reach out to those you know and find new people to share your time with. There are plenty of organizations, charities and clubs that would make you feel welcome. If the

feeling of loneliness is overwhelming,
do please seek help from your doctor.

◆ Learn to enjoy your own company.
Reframe the negative and see time alone
as a positive – listen to music you love,
meditate, go for a walk while listening to
a podcast or read a book. Embrace the
quiet moments rather than fearing them.

◆ Don't be afraid to have solo adventures.
Whether it's to the cinema, the theatre,
a spa hotel or holiday abroad, never let
the thought of a stranger judging you
hold you back from doing what you
want. Be confident in your choice to
spend time alone.

Before I go...

I hope you've enjoyed The Friendship Formula, and that it's given you the motivation to look at your friendship circles, give them a spring clean, see who brings you joy, recognize the mood hoovers and make more effort with those you love.

Friendship is an absolute gift and we should never take a good friend for granted. I hope this book has empowered you to cut out anyone toxic in your life, reassess anyone bringing negativity to the party and truly embrace your inner circle.

If I've learnt anything from my friends over four decades it's to always tell those closest to you how much they mean to you, never hesitate to say 'I love you' and try to be there in their hour of need. Because you never know when someone can be taken away.

Learn to love time alone, surround yourself with positive people who make you feel like the wonderful person you are. The people you choose to spend time with should multiply your happiness. Never forget – you are worthy of the best friendships and people who make you feel fabulous.

Your friend,

Caroline

x

Associations and more information

Katie Haines Memorial Trust
katiehainestrust.com

Macmillan Cancer Support
macmillan.org.uk

Pancreatic Cancer Action
pancreaticcanceraction.org

Cruse Bereavement Care
cruse.org.uk

Social networking services; loneliness helplines

Campaign to End Loneliness
campaigntoendloneliness.org

Nextdoor
nextdoor.com

Meetup
meetup.com

Girlfriend Social: Where Women Make New Friends
girlfriendsocial.com

Do-it
do-it.org

MumsMeetUp
mumsmeetup.com

Bumble BFF
bumble.com/bff

Peanut

peanut-app.io

Mush

letsmush.com

The Silver Line

Helpline: 0800 4 70 80 90
thesilverline.org.uk

Mind

MindInfoline: 0300 123 3393
mind.org.uk

Contributors

Annabelle Knight – annabelleknight.com

Charlie O'Brien – charlieobrien.co.uk

Andy Langford, chief operating officer at Cruse
Bereavement Care – cruse.org.uk

Jo Wimble-Groves – guiltymother.co.uk

Thank yous

Firstly, thank YOU for reading *The Friendship Formula*. I hope you've enjoyed it and will be making sure you get the most out of all your friendships in future.

A huge thanks to my agent Carly Cook and editor Ellen Parnavelas and all the team at Head of Zeus for your patience and encouragement.

To Avril and Gordon Samuel and Richard Haines for allowing me to write about the beautiful Katie. I am forever grateful she was my friend. And big thanks to Leesa Reeve-Daniels for letting me write about Gavin, a man with an incredible spirit. Katie and Gavin will always hold a special place in my heart. Also thank you to Karen Hyland for giving her blessing to share our grief for Katie.

Thanks to Annabelle, Jo and Charlie for your contributions and support. Thanks to Cruse Bereavement Care for their advice about loss and grief. And to everyone who took part in the Friendship Formula survey, thank you for your input and sharing such personal stories.

To my family: Mum and Dad, for your love and support in all I do, and patience when I disappear to write for months. I love you both. Leanne, my big sister and best friend in the world. There are not enough thank yous in the world – superglue forever. Jake and Eliza, I love you as big as the universe and to the moon and back.

My best friends: Ruth and Dave Vernon, James and Edward for your decades of friendship. You are the family I choose for myself. Here's to the next twenty years and the rest... Ian Walker, Jessica, Katie and Joe. Nearly three decades and we're still teenagers at heart. I love you all.

To my 'inner circle': 'Whitstable and beyond' and 'Jen,Je,Ca,Ash,Eri,Ka'. Thanks for your patience while I wrote this and wasn't available to come out and play. To all the cheerleaders in my life, particularly Jessica Bowden, Frankie Seaman, Matt Evers, Gemma Oaten, all the members of Monday Night Club and the fabulous Dibley gang. Also, the ex-Nowies, Camilla Sacre-Dallerup, and Donna Armstrong for your friendship, the Bali Bliss girls and my favourite photographer Nicky Johnston. And to all my friends who I've drunk gin with, sung karaoke and danced til the wee hours with. Thank you!

Special thanks to Nick Boulos for coming up with the title of this book and being a constant source of inspiration and love. Pinky and Perky forever.

And finally, to all the people who have been my friends over the years – thanks for the lessons you've taught me.